# ABUNDANCE

*Your Path Starts Here*

# ABUNDANCE

*Your Path Starts Here*

K E N D A L L    K I N G

CURRENTE
MEDIA
NEW YORK

ISBN: 978-0-9997059-0-2

For bulk orders of this Currente title, contact
Currente Media
Currente-Calamo LLC
244 Fifth Avenue, Suite D169
New York, N.Y. 10001
info@currentemedia.com

*This book is dedicated to Courtney, Austin, and Tanner.*

# TABLE OF CONTENTS

Introduction ................................................................ 1

CHAPTER 1
Never Invest Money Without a Specific Goal............................ 7

CHAPTER 2
Taking Stock: Stocks and Other Asset Classes ........................ 23

CHAPTER 3
Everybody Takes Risk.................................................... 43

CHAPTER 4
An Investor's Theory of Time .......................................... 55

CHAPTER 5
The Smart Investor's Nearly Free Lunch:
Delicious Diversification .............................................. 67

CHAPTER 6
The Well-Timed Pause: Often the Best
Thing to Do Is...Nothing............................................... 85

CHAPTER 7
The Enemies Within.................................................... 93

CHAPTER 8
Your Secret Weapon: Your Advisor.................................... 109

CHAPTER 9
The Sullenberger Lesson: How to Plan for the Unexpected..... 127

CHAPTER 10
Finding Enough: A Chance for the Better ........................... 135

CHAPTER 11
The Well-Balanced Second Life: Maximizing
Your Life's Potential.................................................. 149

FINAL THOUGHTS .................................................... 161

ABOUT THE AUTHOR................................................ 166

SOURCE INFORMATION ............................................ 167

# INTRODUCTION

# YOUR PATH TO ABUNDANCE STARTS HERE

**You are here:** If you want to reach abundance, you are in the right place. The best way to start on the path to abundance is through informed investing, so begin by investing a little time with this book. That's my first word of advice.

I invested my own time in writing this book for three reasons:

**1. To teach people an investment philosophy proven to be successful.** We live in an incredibly fast-moving world filled with the greatest technology ever seen. Unfortunately, this can make investing increasingly complicated and confusing for the average person. I've been very fortunate to have had some great successes in my 15 years as a financial advisor, and I've made a few highly educational mistakes, too. My advice has helped my clients, and I'd like to help more people on a broader level. This book will make that possible.

**2. Because many people could live much more *abundant* lives through their investments.** That's what my firm's purpose is: *to help people achieve abundance.* What we mean by that is this: you want to invest to make a great return, but ultimately you're doing that for a reason—to lead the life you desire, to create abundance in your life. I think that many more people can get what they need to live abundantly, even if they don't always see that as a possibility for themselves.

**3. Most people don't have access to good advice.** A lot of people fail to get where they want to go with their money—mostly,

I believe, amid the confusion created by having so many options available out there. So where can they turn for advice? The internet? I don't think so. Seeking money advice online makes every click a risk. Meanwhile, Wall Street is constantly changing its tune on how to invest. The media cover business and finance as if they're entertainment but rarely get down to helping people make solid, sober decisions. The press mostly seems to want to get you anxious: after all, that's how subscriptions sell. But this causes people to make poor decisions without thinking through things.

I hope someone out there will read this book and say, "This book gives me a philosophy, a guideline for how to make my investment decisions." You might think that you need to seek still more technical expertise—and you'd be right—but at least you're not going to blindly fall in line with whatever most people do. You're going to go your own way, the way you know is best for you, and not follow the herd. That's the first big step toward understanding the basics of investing.

I got into financial advising because I was fascinated by finance and markets. Eventually I realized that I was even more intrigued by the unlimited opportunity to help people by making a positive impact on their lives. Usually money and emotions don't mix, but I realized that the emotional side was what was really calling me to this profession. I had learned to intimately understand a range of financial theories and principles, and that was great—but the battle for security and abundance is won or lost in people's hearts. Fighting that battle is what drives me every day.

**My Backstory:** When my wife's father died, at 49, he left his wife and four daughters, aged 10 to 20. Fortunately, he had been wise beyond his years—smart enough to think *Hey, if I'm not here, my* *family's going to be in major trouble, because I'm the main breadwinner.* In the wake of his death his wife received life insurance proceeds. When trying to decide what to do with them, she turned to someone she thought she could trust.

The Wall Street broker to whom she turned was an acquaintance of the family who wanted to show her how to invest her money. But despite his good intentions, he ended up giving poor advice (all the while collecting heavy commissions and fees). To make matters worse, he came on the scene during the Y2K tech bubble, whose burst hit a lot of the US stock market very severely. Unfortunately for my mother-in-law, he put a lot of her money into technology stocks—and, as a result, lost over half of it. That would be devastating for anyone, but for a widowed mother of four, it was especially difficult. At the time, I was dating her oldest child, my future wife, and soon after that we got engaged. The painful experience my wife's family went through affected me deeply, creating a special place in my heart for widows and other people who don't know where to turn for financial advice.

Many of my clients have had difficult experiences similar to my mother-in-law's. One, a very successful executive—who makes plenty of money and could have started on his journey to abundance much sooner—was reluctant even to come to me. He didn't really trust anybody, because he had watched his parents get taken advantage of by a broker who sold them a bunch of high-commission investments, leaving them in a less than ideal financial situation. He and I eventually developed a connection early in my career. It was a great experience, because it was pretty incredible that he trusted me, a young advisor just starting out, to take him through a financial investment plan that gave him the ability to retire from a very demanding job. What had started out as a painful relationship with financial advisors ended in a positive and productive experience. My dream is for every person to experience this type of relationship with his or her financial advisor.

**Is this book for you?** Probably, since this book is for any investor who wants to achieve abundance in life through investments. I intend it to be useful for every interested reader, but people in their 40s or older may find it most helpful. There is something about turning age 50 that causes people to become more open to creating a retirement plan.

I hope this book will give you a simple blueprint for achieving your most important investment goals as well as your financial goals more generally—that is, for achieving abundance. In it, I'll explain some important steps you'll need to complete to find a financial advisor, as well as how to set your financial goals. When you set financial goals, at some point you'll be asking yourself, "What is all this money *for?*" Maybe you want to spend your later years working at something that won't pay you a lot—or perhaps that won't pay you anything.

In essence, your money is buying you time: whatever it is you want to be doing, *money can buy you time in which to do it.* Money can also buy stuff and pay for fun experiences, but those are not its most important purposes. Money won't buy happiness on its own, but if you can think about the right way to spend money, it will certainly improve your life.

We live in a time when things are moving very quickly and in which we're surrounded by a sea of information and just plain noise, whether from social media, the 24-hour news cycle, or even grocery store tabloids. News travels extremely quickly nowadays: when something goes wrong on the other side of the planet, it affects the investment world in real time. If you're not careful, you can be overwhelmed by everything that's getting thrown around at such an incredible pace. You need to prioritize the getting of sound advice for achieving the abundance you seek. Without it, you're facing a difficult path indeed.

If I am able to help you, then I'll be all the gladder that you picked up this book. And let me first recognize my fantastic wife, Courtney, as the primary reason I'm writing this book. Without her encouragement and belief in me during my early years as an advisor, I would have given up on my dream many years ago. I also have to note that without my amazing clients, particularly the ones who trusted a 20-something beardless guy, I wouldn't be in this position. I have had the incredible honor of working with many people who have trusted me to guide them—and many of whom are now lifelong friends.

I hope this book connects with you, wherever you are in your financial life, and helps you find the next step you need to take to reach your abundant goals. As you're reading, you might come across several good ideas that apply to you, but if you can just find one idea that really speaks to you, then grab onto that one idea—and take action. If that happens, I'll have achieved my goal in writing this book. And please remember: I'll always be glad to hear from you, happy to help in any way I can.

Kendall King

castleviewadvisors.com

kendall@castleviewadvisors.com

# CHAPTER 1

# NEVER INVEST
# MONEY WITHOUT
# A SPECIFIC GOAL

*Without vision, the people will perish.*
*—Proverbs 29:18*

## A SURFER'S GUIDE TO
## FINANCIAL PLANNING

A beginners' surfing class might not be the most intuitive place to go for financial advice, but it works. Here's the proof:

When I was in Hawaii recently, I learned to surf. Because I live in landlocked Oklahoma City most of the year, surfing was a bit of a challenge. But the first thing the instructor said was, "Okay, here's what we're trying to do: you want to get up on the water, you want to have fun, you want to surf. But to do that, there are steps involved—and *you cannot skip the steps.*"

That was great advice. I learned that whether you're riding a wave or trying to grow your money, you need to go through specific steps. It's easy to try to jump straight to "I'm going to surf" (if by "surf" you mean "adopt the investment plan that will allow me to live the abundant life I desire"). But to do that, it's important to understand the steps involved in getting there. Beyond that, if you don't want to wipe out, you have to follow the steps and discipline yourself to follow them. If you want to be able to ride the waves, you need to have a good handle on the basics.

**If you skip a step or try to pursue some shortcut to getting rich quick, you're going to wipe out.**

**Good form takes planning.** The steps that I learned in that beginners' surfing class were extremely specific, and there are a lot more of them than a nonsurfer would expect. Practiced surfers make the sport seem easy and graceful because they practice each basic step daily, using excellent form every time. They never get ahead of themselves. At one point, the instructor even said to me, "Kendall, I know you're a pretty good athlete, but I'll take form over athleticism every day of the week."

That made me think: Many people can occasionally make a good stock pick, but they do so purely by luck. However, if you have a strong *process* in place—a plan, in other words—and can stay disciplined and focused on the fundamental steps in that process, that discipline is what will give you a greater chance of achieving real success—both in the surf and in your investment plan. That's another thing my surfing instructor really hammered home: "You can't skip any step. If you skip a step, your chances of enjoying surfing go way, way down." The same is true in financial planning and financial discipline. If you skip a step or try to pursue some shortcut to getting rich quick, you're going to wipe out and fall off your figurative board.

Think of great athletes. It doesn't matter which sport they played or when they lived—the characteristic they all share is a constant emphasis on the fundamentals. Tom Brady is a great example of this. Recently, I read an article that examined his off-season training program. He has won the Super Bowl five times and is widely regarded as one of the best quarterbacks in the history of the NFL, but every summer, he goes back to working on the fundamentals, sharpening the basic skills that go into being a great quarterback.

When I read that, it completely changed my view of him. A lot of people, myself included, are ready to say, "Well, Tom Brady doesn't need to work on that stuff; he's already got it all down." But a great performance always starts with the fundamentals—so make sure that you're really, really good at them.

One other very important aspect of Tom Brady's success has to do with his personal coach. The two of them work together with a single objective: to help Tom Brady get even better at playing football, no matter whether he's already the most successful quarterback in the NFL. What is true of Tom Brady is also true of stellar performers in every field; they all have a coach, a mentor, or an advisor.

**Without the fundamentals, you can't be successful.**

This isn't accidental. Even when you're the best at something, you are never too good to go back to working on the basics. You can always improve your fundamental skills, both in sports and in finance, but without the fundamentals, you can't be successful. And without a personal coach to help you along the way, you will never achieve your full potential.

# GOALS: BEYOND THE FOOTBALL FIELD

By my definition, a goal is a dream with a deadline. Often clients come to me and say, "I want to have the option to stop working," but others say "I want to have $100,000 coming into my account every year from passive income by the time I'm 60 years old." The first statement is a dream; the second statement is a goal. Having a specific goal in mind—and a specific time by which you want to achieve it—makes that goal significantly easier to plan for and eventually achieve.

## A GOAL IS A DREAM WITH A DEADLINE

Pilots know the absolute necessity for a flight plan, and so should you. Just as every flight requires a destination, so every decision that you make with your finances must be guided by the plan that will get you there. The goal is not the flight; it's reaching the destination. So here is where we start laying down steps in order. The goal must come first. After that, you can build a plan, and by following your plan, you can determine what goes into your portfolio. But if there is no goal, you're essentially just throwing money around. You need to know what you're trying to achieve. Only then can you get to creating the right financial plan. As you know, that plan includes several things, but it can also be thought of as a plan for action: *How much do I need to save? How do I need to invest that money? What type of accounts do I put it in?* Only after following these steps can you find the right portfolio, deciding what investments you're going to hold and how you're going to fund your financial plan.

---

**BENCHMARKS**

When I talk to clients about benchmarks, I always stress that everyone is unique. The only benchmark that really matters is whether, when you're reviewing your investment plan and reviewing your returns and savings, you are on track to meet your goal. Remember: The benchmark that matters is not how your portfolio performs in comparison to the Dow Jones Industrial Average. Stop looking at all the benchmarks you see on the television or read about in the news. Your financial plan should be made up of personalized benchmarks suited to your goals specifically. What matters is how your portfolio performs in reaching those.

---

> **The fundamental goal is to create an abundant life, to your definition of abundance, on your timescale.**

The fundamental goal for us here is to create an abundant life, by your definition of abundance and on your timescale. That said, it's good to try to keep your goals realistic but also not to sell yourself short. A lot of people don't understand how to strike that balance.

The goals we're talking about are not only return-driven, nor are they guided by external factors such as the economy or the latest geopolitical crisis. As an example, the portfolio of our fictitious investor, Joe, often outperforms the S&P 500, but he is not on track to meet his financial goals. Andy's portfolio, by contrast, has been well thought-out to fund his personal financial goals and is more suitable to his risk preferences, allowing him to reach his goals—even though his portfolio rarely outperforms Joe's.

## THREE EXAMPLES OF ABUNDANCE GOALS

- Having a retirement income stream that you will never outlive

- Making sure your kids or your grandkids come out of college without any student debt

- Being able to give $100,000 to your favorite church or charity on your death—or, better yet, while you are still living

It seems pretty clear to me that Andy is the winner here. Joe's portfolio might have outperformed the S&P 500 in most years, *but he still hasn't achieved his goals.* By the same token, your goals should not be arbitrary; they should be specific and important to you.

Setting specific goals can be difficult, especially if you try to do it right off the bat. I've found that it's often helpful to think first of your vision for your life. The other day, I was talking to a client whom we'll call Andrea. Andrea was struggling to formulate a solid goal and pin down a timeline when I finally asked her, "What's your vision for your life?"

## GOALS THROUGH TIME

It's worth noting that by the time people become my clients, they are usually already in their 40s or 50s. Although this book is written with that in mind, if someone younger is reading it and taking this advice to heart, you're ahead of the curve. It's hard to think about something like retirement at age 25 or even 35, but the earlier you can get your goals in place, the better off you are.

All that said, when we're planning financial goals, they should be flexible to some degree. For example, a younger family might have financial goals such as purchasing a larger house to accommodate their family's growth or ensuring that their children graduate college free of debt rather than saving for the parents' retirement. Contrast this with an older couple who have adult children living outside the home: that couple is probably thinking more about retirement, or perhaps about downsizing their living space, than about getting a bigger place.

The key to handling changing goals is to reassess them on a regular basis. We tell our clients to sit down for an annual checkup and think through their goals: Are your goals still what we have down? Has your goal, your vision, changed? Goals can also shift because of changing circumstances and family events, which may accelerate some goals or put the brakes on others. More often than not, however, your goals will remain the same, requiring only minor tweaks from year to year.

That helped her out a lot. She had plenty of vision for how she wanted her life to be, which included traveling the world as well as visiting her out-of-town grandchildren several times a year. Because of that clarity, we were able to start from her vision and work our way through the more quantitative aspects of how her goal would work. *When considering your goals, don't neglect the vision you have for how you want your life to be.* That vision is going to help you figure out what living abundantly means for you.

## HOW TO BUILD YOUR GOALS

The first thing to consider is what your eventual passive income goal is. Passive income is not income you have to go out and earn; rather, it comes from investments. It can be a source of retirement income to supplement your mailbox income (Social Security, pension, rental income, etc.). Many of your other goals will either supplement that goal or pertain to the lifestyle you want—in other words, what you want to do with that income goal. Everybody is different: for some people, focusing on a certain income goal will come easily. While others will have to reflect on what they want and then figure out how much they will need to bring in to support the vision they have for their life together.

Regardless of whether you can easily summon that number or you need to deduce it from current spending and prospective costs of other goals, you still need a number to shoot for. The level of specificity will change as you get older. If you're setting your goals at age 35, you can aim for a ballpark figure, but if you're 60, you need to have something very specific in mind.

# SET REALISTIC GOALS

Let's say that you are 50 years old with $250,000 in your investment accounts. Your goal is to have a $500,000 annual retirement income coming your way starting at age 60. But right now you're saving only $500 a month. That half-million-dollar income is not realistic. But if your goal is to have a retirement income of $50,000 per year, saving $500 a month may give you a great chance to achieve that goal.

> **Being realistic about your earning and saving capabilities is the key to creating an achievable goal.**

Being realistic about your earning and saving capabilities is the key to creating an achievable goal. All people are different in their ability to produce income and ability to save.

For example, suppose that a new client comes into our office: a single woman, 55 years old. She says, "Kendall, I have $1,000,000, and I want to retire in five years. I want to be able to bring in $60,000 a year from my investments. Make it happen."

That's a goal we can work with. For my part, I'll use her goal to look into what investment return is needed to achieve that goal. When I look at what return we need to get and see that the return needs to be 7 percent for example, that is very achievable. But if we do the math and it shows that we need an 18 percent return, I have to tell the client to lower his or her income goal, to work longer, or to contribute much more aggressively to his or her retirement accounts. In the case of this hypothetical client, her annual return need be only 6 percent to achieve her goal, which is realistic.

# THE THREE KEYS TO UNLOCKING ABUNDANCE

We can find abundance in our financial plans in many ways. After you've set your goal and figured out your plan of action, there are three keys ways to find abundance on your path.

**The first key is your advisor.** Most people will have no chance of reaching the abundant goal they have set without the help of a competent, trustworthy, caring financial advisor. *If there is one investment mistake that you can't afford to make, it's that of hiring the wrong advisor.* An advisor not only will help you make smart choices, but he or she will also help keep your emotions about your money in check. It's very easy to panic during market turmoil, especially when you're close to retirement, and an advisor will provide discipline and behavior coaching to calm those heightened feelings.

> **The Keys to Reaching Abundance**
> 1. Your advisor
> 2. Your stocks
> 3. Your long-term perspective

**The second key is stocks.** Stocks are not just pieces of paper or electronic tickers on the computer; these are certificates of ownership in real companies that manufacture things, provide services, hire people, produce earnings, and create dividends based on profits. A major part of your plan needs to include how much of your money will be allocated to stocks. Most of my clients, when they first come to me, frequently don't allocate enough of their investment accounts to stocks. Stocks have a reputation for being too risky for people who are close to retirement, but they can actually *decrease* the risk of your retirement plan. (Much more on this later.)

> Our society wants to focus on what's going on today, but a great investor takes a much longer view than today, this week, or even this year.

**The third key is a long-term perspective**, almost a historical perspective. As Winston Churchill said, "The further you look back, the further you can look forward." It's important to keep in mind that this year is just one year in a plan designed to last for years. Amid the 24-hour news cycle and social media, it's more difficult than ever before to have a long-term perspective. Our society wants to focus on what's going on today, or even this minute, but a great investor takes a much longer view than today, this week, or even this year.

Ignoring these keys can lead to very scattered portfolios as well as to microscopic views of the state of the market. I always hear people say, "I want to make sure that I get this right—that I don't invest money just when stocks are about to go down sharply." A goal isn't trying to figure out what direction the market is going, or timing your investments correctly for the next week or month. It's projecting what the market will do over many years in the future. That's why the third key is there.

By the same token, a goal is not trying to do better than your neighbor. After all, what do your goals have to do with your neighbors? Trying to do better than others, and indeed comparing yourself to others in any way, can lead to goals that just aren't useful. I often have clients come to me and say something such as "I need three million dollars to retire." When I ask where that number came from, I almost always hear, "I know a smart guy, and he told me that you need three million dollars to retire." A goal has nothing to do with other people.

It has everything to do with you and the unique, individual, important goals that will help you pursue an abundant vision for your life. When we set goals, all we're doing is putting a dollar value on that vision.

> **A goal has nothing to do with other people. It has everything to do with you.**

If your goals are poorly defined and you don't have a timeline and a plan of action in place for achieving them, they're never going to happen. Remember Joe and Andy from earlier in the chapter? Joe wanted to outperform the S&P 500, but even if that happens, he still might not achieve his real visions for his life. He never really established a goal. Andy, by contrast, had a specific goal, a timeline, and a plan of action for achieving it. If Joe had come to me with that goal at this point in my career, I would have had to either tell him that a partnership between us would not work out or sit down with him and work out a better goal.

Here's a great example of what setting yourself up for success looks like. Recently I took on a new client whom we'll call Cindy. Cindy is 58 years old and recently went through a divorce. She has $1,500,000 to put toward her goals. She knows what her vision for her life is: she's going back to work, but her goal is to be able to

> **If your goals are poorly defined and you don't have a timeline and a plan of action in place for achieving them, they're never going to happen.**

stop working within three years and travel the world, drink good wine and play some golf. She also wants to be able to make a significant contribution to Catholic charities, supporting their good works and the maintenance of their churches.

---

### CROSSING THE FINISH LINE

A goal is very important, but it's useful only if you have a specific plan of action. A long time ago, my dad set a goal of running the Boston Marathon, which is a very clear, specific goal. In his case, that meant that he needed a training plan, and not just any training plan. He needed the right training plan to get his body ready for running that race. He had to qualify for the Boston Marathon, which meant that he had to run a qualifying marathon beforehand and finish it in a specific time, or he wouldn't be able to take part in the Boston Marathon. So in 1989, he said, "I'm going to run the Boston Marathon in 1991." He established a timeline, placed a deadline on his dream, and—to his credit—achieved it. *The ability to set goals and stick to them is a skill that is important in many aspects of our lives.*

---

Together, we sat down and did the math. To support the lifestyle she wants for her retirement, she needs $75,000 per year. We worked together to find a way to turn her $1,500,000 into a passive income to support her for many years to come. Cindy came to me with exciting but realistic dreams as well as a realistic timeframe in which achieve them. She's well on her way to the life she wants to lead.

# THE NONABUNDANT WAY
# VERSUS THE ABUNDANT WAY

The points we've covered in this chapter all work together. Setting a goal and following your financial plan are essentially exercises in discipline, in keeping a cool head in spite of whatever might be going on in the news. What usually gets people in trouble—and we'll return to this in future chapters—is basing decisions on emotions instead of on plans and goals.

When I get a call from a client saying, "Hey, I looked at what's going on in the markets. Should we change things in my portfolio?" my first question will always be, "Well, let me ask you this: *have your goals changed?*"

If the client says no—and most do—then my next question is, "Okay. Has there been a major life change for you that I don't know about?" If the client says no to that, too, then I say, "The best thing for us to do is exactly what we are already doing, changing nothing instead of reacting." Acting on your plan is the key, as opposed to reacting to world or market events.

Nonabundant wisdom follows an often unwise path: Invest your money into a random mix of investments. Don't keep track of your goals or make a financial plan; you'll figure it out eventually. The movement of the market today, or this week, or this month, is the final arbiter of your success.

> **Act based on your fundamentals—your goal, your plan, your deadline—rather than reacting to mass hysterias.**

The abundant way, by contrast, is very different. Set specific goals. Create a well-thought-out financial plan with the help of a trusted and competent financial advisor. Select your investments based solely on your financial plan rather than on what the CNBC talking head is telling you to do right now. *Take as long a view as you can.*

| THE NONABUNDANT WAY | THE ABUNDANT WAY |
|---|---|
| Never create a vision or take time to think about your future goals. | Create a vision for your future, setting your goals before doing anything else. |
| Invest in a lot of different things before creating a plan. | Create a well-thought-out financial plan before making investment decisions. |
| Don't view your choice of an advisor as critical. | Choose your advisor carefully, selecting one whom you can trust and who understands you. |

# CHAPTER 2

# TAKING STOCK: STOCKS AND OTHER ASSET CLASSES

*My favorite holding period is forever.*
—Warren Buffett

## STOCK ANSWERS

If I could pinpoint the biggest mistake that investors make, the thing that causes them *not* to achieve their goals, it is that most people don't own enough stocks in their investment plan—or, if they do, they don't hold them for long enough. Many people simply don't own as many stocks as they should.

When you think of stocks and bonds, think of owning a business versus lending to a business. If you are the owner of a business—let's say it's a widget business—you get all the upside and profits of this widget business, but you also get all the potential losses. This is what a stock is. The lender to your business (let's say it's your aunt) would essentially own a bond on your business. She does not share in the profits, but she is promised to be paid an interest rate by you for her loan. Her upside is limited to the interest rate promised. She does not share in the downside of your company. Her risk is only that of your defaulting on your interest payments. Now you understand the difference between a stock and bond.

## STOCKS AND BONDS ARE CONDUITS FOR CAPITAL

Bondholders are lenders to a company.
Stockholders are equity owners in the business.
Both expect an adequate return for the
terms and risk of their investment.

Let's examine each asset class in terms of risks and benefits.

**1. Stock risks.** We'll be discussing a few different asset classes in this chapter, as well as the differences between them. I'll get into bonds and alternative assets as well, but my primary focus is on stocks. In my view, stocks are the key to future abundance, for a variety of reasons. Remember, stocks are not just a ticker or a piece of paper. When you own stock in a business, you personally own part of that business—maybe not a big part, but a real part, and it's yours, which means you have a claim on all future profits and distributions.

**The Four Major Asset Classes**

1. **Stocks**
2. **Bonds**
3. **Cash**
4. **Alternatives**

With stocks, the biggest risk tends to be the potential for short-term loss or fluctuation of principal. The benefit of stocks, on the other hand, is that they have the highest expected return. This is primarily due to their potential for larger capital appreciation as the company's value and price go up. Additionally, you will typically benefit from quarterly dividend payments that rise over time because of the dividends they pay along the way. Stocks also have the potential for larger capital gains over time as company stock prices go up. If you hold them long enough, you're going to benefit from the dividend income as well as the capital gains.

**2. Bond risks.** We've already mentioned one of the biggest risks attached to bonds: default. Bonds also have risk attached because of their sensitivity to interest rates. The interest rate of bonds is typically fixed, so as interest rates move up, the relative value of a bond may go down because the rate was fixed in the beginning. For example, let's say you buy a bond paying a 3 percent yield in the current environment—which would be pretty good—and interest rates rise in the next year so that this same type of bond is paying 4 percent. That would cause your bond to lose value due to a lower-than-current-market interest rate.

Another risk with bonds, and indeed perhaps the biggest one, is the potential loss of purchasing power—your ability to spend money in the future as you are spending it today. If you own a bond and the fixed return does not keep up with inflation (and these days it rarely does), you could lose purchasing power.

Because people do business around the world, a world of opportunity is out there waiting for you to discover it. Here's an example:

# DIVERSIFICATION HELPS YOU CAPTURE
# WHAT GLOBAL MARKETS OFFER

Percent of world market capitalization as of December 31, 2016

■ DEVELOPED MARKETS  ■ EMERGING MARKETS  ■ FRONTIER MARKETS

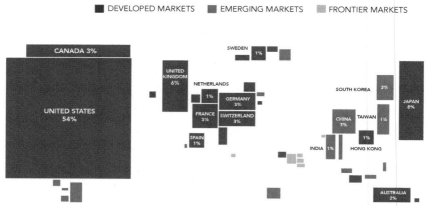

The global equity market is large and represents a world of investment opportunity.

# THERE'S A WORLD OF OPPORTUNITY
# IN FIXED INCOME

Percent of global investment grade bond market as of December 31, 2016

■ GOVERNMENT  ■ CORPORATE

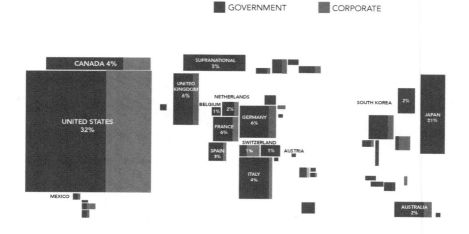

A bond, unlike a stock, is essentially a loan. The difference is that instead of taking out a loan from a bank, a company sells bonds. A bond is a fixed-income investment, and the rate is set at a specific number.

The biggest benefit of bonds is that they are a great way to smooth the ride of a portfolio that is mostly invested in stocks while also generating a reliable source of income. This is much more important for investors in retirement, especially when going through the stock downturns that will happen periodically.

**3. Cash risks.** Cash is the most straightforward asset class. Savings accounts, checking accounts, CDs, money market accounts, and Treasury bills are all considered cash or cash equivalents. When you have a cash investment, you receive a fixed interest on the money you have in that investment. The interest is typically very low in comparison to that available for other asset classes, particularly in today's low–interest rate environment. In fact, the return is often much lower than inflation.

The most important upside of cash is that it essentially has no risk of losing principal. This is especially true if you have FDIC coverage on your savings account or CD, which means that the government will step in and guarantee that you won't lose that money. Cash also provides the comfort factor. For some people, knowing that they have a certain amount of cash makes them more comfortable taking on other risks, including stock market risk. It's also important to have enough cash earmarked for short-term needs.

However, the biggest risk of holding cash is essentially the same risk incurred by holding bonds, but to a much greater degree: By holding too much cash, you are slowly becoming less wealthy.

Inflation will be there every year, and if you're getting 1 percent or less on your cash, there is a real risk that inflation will eat up your returns. It will drive down your purchasing power, and it may keep you from reaching your goals.

**It may keep you from reaching your goals.**

## THE CAPITAL MARKETS HAVE REWARDED LONG-TERM INVESTORS

Monthly Growth of Wealth ($1), 1926-2016

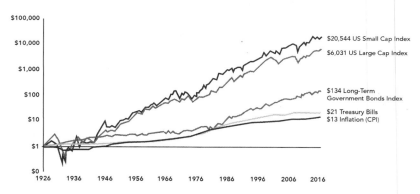

**4. Alternative assets risks.** Most people should avoid alternative assets, such as gold and other commodities, unless they want to speculate. Hedge funds and private equity funds are also forms of alternative assets. There are many others, but these are the most common, and each comes with a unique set of risks. If you go into the global market to buy a stock in, say, Peru, you're also buying into the promise of future Peruvian stability.

---

**WHAT IS A HEDGE FUND?**

A hedge fund is similar to a mutual fund, but the manager of the fund is free to do things that a regular person can't do and can even do a number of things that a mutual fund manager can't do. For example, a hedge fund manager can essentially make a bet that European currency will go up.

---

# BONDS 101

There are many different types of bonds, but I'm going to explain a little bit about the four main types of bonds: US government bonds, municipal bonds, corporate bonds, and foreign (or non-US) bonds.

**1. Government bonds.** When you own a US government bond, also known as a Treasury bond, you are loaning money to the US government. These tend to be the safest types of bonds,

### The Four Types of Bonds
1. US Government Bonds
2. Municipal Bonds
3. Corporate bonds
4. International bonds

because they're backed by the full faith and credit of the US government. They have the strongest backing and the lowest risk of default. The US government has never yet defaulted on a bond; it has a very strong history of making sure that you get your money back when you buy a bond.

The biggest problem with the US government bond is that for the extra assurance of getting paid, the rates tend to be lower than for other types of bonds. In exchange for the closest thing to a guarantee you're going to find in the world of bonds, you also have a lower rate of return. For most people who buy bonds, US government bonds should be the largest part of their bond holding. If the goal in owning bonds is to dampen the fluctuations of a portfolio and to ensure that the portfolio owner never has to worry about short-term risk so long as the United States is around, Treasury bonds should make up the largest portion of the bond portfolio. It's also worth noting that US government bonds are taxable at the federal level but not the state.

> **The biggest problem with the US government bond is that for the extra assurance of getting paid, the rates tend to be lower than for other types of bonds.**

**2. Municipal bonds**, as their name suggests, are issued by states, cities, and municipalities. Just as with corporate bonds, municipal bonds can have different grades and different values. They are issued to cover needs that those areas have, such as by paying for a big water project, a new highway, a major dam, or just about anything else for which the municipality needs to raise money. These bonds are usually the safest after US government bonds. There is a very low default rate on municipal bonds.

The biggest benefit of municipal bonds is that they are tax-free at the federal level. Remember—not even US government bonds are tax-free for federal purposes. Municipal bonds are also free of tax at the state level if you buy bonds in your state of residency. This makes municipal bonds very useful for people to own if they're in a high tax bracket and are investing money from a taxable account rather than, say, an IRA.

**3. Corporate bonds** are another common type of bond. Strong corporations, such as Exxon, Apple, and Walmart, tend to have very high-quality corporate bonds. When you hold a corporate bond, you're loaning money to a corporation. The interest rate for corporate bonds does tend to be higher than the rate for US government bonds—even a lot higher if you are willing to take on a bond from a less-than-stellar corporation, knowing that the weaker a company is, the lower its creditworthiness—meaning that investors get a higher interest rate to hold the company's bond in exchange for a greater risk of default. If you find a super-high interest rate among corporate bonds, you have started buying what are called junk bonds (also known as high-yield bonds), which carry extra risks. Most bond investors should avoid junk bonds if they want their bonds to stabilize a portfolio.

The best way to understand how strong different corporate or municipal bonds are is to look at the major credit agencies that rate these bonds: Standard and Poor's, for example, or Moody's. All corporations or municipalities have a rating on the trustworthiness of their bonds, which can be as high as Aaa/AAA and as low as CCC.

| Definition | Moodys | S&P | Fitch |
|---|---|---|---|
| **Investment Grade** | | | |
| Prime, maximum safety | Aaa | AAA | AAA |
| Very high grade/quality | Aa1 | AA+ | AA+ |
| " | Aa2 | AA | AA |
| " | Aa1 | AA- | AA- |
| Upper medium quality | A1 | A+ | A+ |
| " | A2 | A | A |
| " | A3 | A- | A- |
| Lower medium grade | Baa1 | BBB+ | BBB+ |
| " | Baa2 | BBB | BBB |
| " | Baa3 | BBB- | BBB- |
| Definition | Moodys | S&P | Fitch |
| **Speculative Grade** | | | |
| Speculative | Ba1 | BB+ | BB+ |
| " | Ba2 | BB | BB |
| " | Ba3 | BB- | BB- |
| Highly speculative | B1 | B+ | B+ |
| " | B2 | B | B |
| " | B3 | B- | B- |
| Substantial risk | Caa1 | CCC+ | CCC+ |
| In poor standing | Caa2 | CCC | CCC |
| " | Caa3 | CCC- | CCC- |
| Extremely speculative | Ca | CC | CC |
| Maybe in or extremely close to default | C | C+,C,C- | C+,C,C- |
| Default | | D | D |

Governments also receive investment grades. In August 2011, Standard and Poor's downgraded the US government debt from its top rating for the first time. But investment grades such as this are generally more useful for nongovernment bonds so long as your government bonds are in a stable country, such as the United States or Japan.

The reason corporate bonds are riskier than government bonds is simple: Corporations can't do the things that the US government can do. A corporation that seems strong now might not be as strong five years from now. Lehman Brothers Holdings was the fourth-largest investment banking firm in the United States, but in 2008, after 150 years in business, it went bankrupt, leaving bondholders high and dry. When you own corporate bonds, you have to keep an eye on the ratings and the health of the company.

**4. International bonds** are just what they say they are: bonds issued by non-US governments. Different countries' bonds have different ratings: holding a German government bond is very different from holding a Russian bond. International bonds are also graded by the rating agencies. The key thing to remember with international bonds is that there is a diversification benefit when you invest outside the United States. For example, in the wake of 2016's Brexit, if you were a British citizen who owned only UK bonds, you'd be in for a rough time, whereas if you owned both British and US bonds, you would have come out much stronger for having diversified your bond exposure. Although international bonds are taxable at the state and federal levels, some do create eligibility for a foreign tax credit.

By a wide margin, the majority of defaults are preceded by downgrades to the issuer's credit rating. See the following chart: AAA-rated entities have not had any defaults, which is no surprise. As you might expect, the lower you go in the credit ratings to pursue a higher yield, the greater your risk of default. Congrats—you now have completed Bonds 101!

| Global Corporate Annual Default Rates By Rating Category (%) | | | | | | |
|---|---|---|---|---|---|---|
| | **AAA** | **AA** | **A** | **BBB** | **BB** | **B** | **CCC/C** |
| 1981 | 0.00 | 0.00 | 0.00 | 0.00 | 0.00 | 2.27 | 0.00 |
| 1982 | 0.00 | 0.00 | 0.21 | 0.34 | 4.22 | 3.13 | 21.43 |
| 1983 | 0.00 | 0.00 | 0.00 | 0.32 | 1.16 | 4.58 | 6.67 |
| 1984 | 0.00 | 0.00 | 0.00 | 0.66 | 1.14 | 3.41 | 25.00 |
| 1985 | 0.00 | 0.00 | 0.00 | 0.00 | 1.48 | 6.47 | 15.38 |
| 1986 | 0.00 | 0.00 | 0.18 | 0.33 | 1.31 | 8.36 | 23.08 |
| 1987 | 0.00 | 0.00 | 0.00 | 0.00 | 0.38 | 3.08 | 12.28 |
| 1988 | 0.00 | 0.00 | 0.00 | 0.00 | 1.05 | 3.63 | 20.37 |
| 1989 | 0.00 | 0.00 | 0.18 | 0.60 | 0.72 | 3.38 | 33.33 |
| 1990 | 0.00 | 0.00 | 0.00 | 0.58 | 3.57 | 8.56 | 31.25 |
| 1991 | 0.00 | 0.00 | 0.00 | 0.55 | 1.69 | 13.84 | 33.87 |
| 1992 | 0.00 | 0.00 | 0.00 | 0.00 | 0.00 | 6.99 | 30.19 |
| 1993 | 0.00 | 0.00 | 0.00 | 0.00 | 0.70 | 2.62 | 13.33 |
| 1994 | 0.00 | 0.00 | 0.14 | 0.00 | 0.28 | 3.08 | 16.67 |
| 1995 | 0.00 | 0.00 | 0.00 | 0.17 | 0.99 | 4.58 | 28.00 |
| 1996 | 0.00 | 0.00 | 0.00 | 0.00 | 0.45 | 2.91 | 8.00 |
| 1997 | 0.00 | 0.00 | 0.00 | 0.25 | 0.19 | 3.51 | 12.00 |
| 1998 | 0.00 | 0.00 | 0.00 | 0.41 | 0.82 | 4.63 | 42.86 |
| 1999 | 0.00 | 0.17 | 0.18 | 0.20 | 0.95 | 7.29 | 33.33 |
| 2000 | 0.00 | 0.00 | 0.27 | 0.37 | 1.15 | 7.67 | 35.96 |
| 2001 | 0.00 | 0.00 | 0.27 | 0.34 | 2.94 | 11.52 | 45.45 |
| 2002 | 0.00 | 0.00 | 0.00 | 1.02 | 2.88 | 8.20 | 44.44 |
| 2003 | 0.00 | 0.00 | 0.00 | 0.23 | 0.58 | 4.06 | 32.73 |
| 2004 | 0.00 | 0.00 | 0.08 | 0.00 | 0.43 | 1.45 | 16.18 |
| 2005 | 0.00 | 0.00 | 0.00 | 0.07 | 0.31 | 1.74 | 9.09 |
| 2006 | 0.00 | 0.00 | 0.00 | 0.00 | 0.30 | 0.82 | 13.33 |
| 2007 | 0.00 | 0.00 | 0.00 | 0.00 | 0.20 | 0.25 | 15.24 |
| 2008 | 0.00 | 0.38 | 0.39 | 0.49 | 0.81 | 4.08 | 27.00 |
| 2009 | 0.00 | 0.00 | 0.22 | 0.55 | 0.75 | 10.92 | 49.46 |
| 2010 | 0.00 | 0.00 | 0.00 | 0.00 | 0.58 | 0.85 | 22.73 |
| 2011 | 0.00 | 0.00 | 0.00 | 0.07 | 0.00 | 1.66 | 16.42 |
| 2012 | 0.00 | 0.00 | 0.00 | 0.00 | 0.30 | 1.56 | 27.33 |
| 2013 | 0.00 | 0.00 | 0.00 | 0.00 | 0.09 | 1.63 | 24.18 |
| 2014 | 0.00 | 0.00 | 0.00 | 0.00 | 0.00 | 0.77 | 17.03 |

# STOCKS VERSUS FIXED RATES

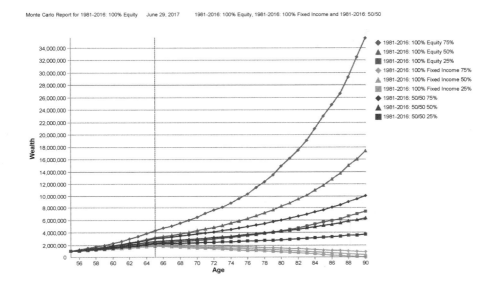

Monte Carlo Report for 1981-2016: 100% Equity    June 29, 2017    1981-2016: 100% Equity, 1981-2016: 100% Fixed Income and 1981-2016: 50/50

**Stocks and bonds considered together:** Now let's try to bring this all together with a case study. As an example, suppose that three different 55-year-olds all want to retire at age 65. Let's assume that each can expect to live to age 90, so in essence they have a 35-year timeline. And let's suppose that they are investing $1,000,000 apiece, with $50,000 annual contributions. Their goal? To pull out $100,000 a year at age 65.

Even though they have the same goal, each has a different strategy. Conservative Charlie invested all his money into a 100 percent fixed income plan: bonds. (I'll be using the phrase *fixed income* interchangeably with *bonds* from here on.) Aggressive Andrea invested 100 percent in an equity plan: stocks. But Balanced Brian had 50 percent stocks and 50 percent fixed income. What happened to their incomes at age 65 if they stuck with their plan? And how were they doing at 90? Let's see what happens.

In the 100 percent fixed-income (bond) portfolio, Conservative Charlie's million-dollar portfolio had $1.975 million at age 65, and he had to draw down the portfolio all the way to $386,000 by age 90. Charlie is in trouble if he lives five more years.

In the 100 percent equity portfolio, Andrea had $3.186 million at age 65, or another $1.2 million. What's more, Andrea grew her account to over $14 million by age 80, even though she had been drawing $100,000 a year since age 65. Not only will she have no worries about running out of money if she lives to age 95 or older, but she will also be able to do some amazing things for her family and her legacy. Keep in mind that she started in the same situation as Charlie—but because of the very simple decision to put her money into stocks rather than bonds, she has an extra $14 million at age 90. Her risk paid off: the only money problem she has at 90 is an estate tax issue.

But let's not forget about Balanced Brian, who decided to split his investments 50/50 between stocks and bonds. He was still able to grow his account to $2.617 million by age 65, which is $617,000 *more* than Charlie's 100 percent bond portfolio. Even drawing down $100,000 a year in retirement, by age 90, Brian still has $6 million, which is plenty to get him through an even longer life into his 90s. He could die on the golf course at 100 years of age with plenty of money in the bank. He also is in the enviable position of being able to help his family and create a lasting legacy.

## NOMINAL AND REAL RETURNS

Remember, **nominal return** is the return that you see on your report or statement. If your portfolio earned 7.2 percent on the year, that's what your report shows. But what actually matters is real returns: how much did you earn above and beyond inflation? If your portfolio had a nominal return of 7.2 percent and inflation is 2.5 percent, your real return was 4.7 percent. Being aware of that difference will help you build it into your financial plan.

**Real returns** are the main reason stocks are so important to a robust portfolio. Historically, stocks pay 10 percent nominal and bonds 5 percent nominal—so if inflation is 3 percent, then stocks' real return is 7 percent, compared to only 2 percent for bonds. In addition, stocks tend to be more lightly taxed than bonds. In fact, when compared to cash vehicles, stocks fare even better than they do against bonds.

**Learn from history.** It's important to ask your advisor to join you in looking at the history of how stocks have done against bonds and to understand the nominal returns and the inflationary effects of the consumer price index (CPI). Once you have your numbers, then you can ask what they look like over the past, say, 80 years. And what about real returns? A closer examination might show that, for example, stocks averaged 10 percent growth and bonds 5.5 percent. That example would have stocks doing 4.5 percent better, but when you factor in inflation at, say, 3 percent, now we're looking at 7 percent on stocks against 2.5 percent on fixed income. Learning the history of economic numbers can help you see that—to follow our example—stocks are performing not merely twice as well as bonds but rather nearer three times as well. Here's another way of looking at all this:

## TOTAL REAL RETURN INDEXES

January 1802–December 2013
Past performance is not indicative of future results.

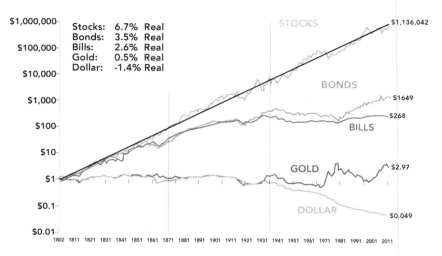

| | |
|---|---|
| Stocks: | 6.7% Real |
| Bonds: | 3.5% Real |
| Bills: | 2.6% Real |
| Gold: | 0.5% Real |
| Dollar: | -1.4% Real |

**Stocks = Abundance.** Based on all the evidence, the more stocks you have, and the longer you hold them, the more abundant your future life will be. It really is that simple. The biggest issue for most people is figuring out how to deal with the short-term uncertainty. The trade-off for future abundance is vulnerability to the things that happen from year to year: 9/11, the 2008 financial crisis, Brexit, and other earth-shaking events undoubtedly yet to come.

# HOW TO BELIEVE IN CAPITALISM

You can't be a great investor if you don't believe in capitalism. That may sound simplistic, perhaps even blunt, but it's something that is important for successful long-term investing.

Under capitalism, as an investor in a company, you're entitled to a share of that company's increase in wealth. That share is called the **capital market rate of return**. In simple terms, if you invest in stocks, you're providing the capital that companies need to reinvest in themselves and thereby increase their returns.

> **It's difficult, if not impossible, to be a great investor if you don't believe in capitalism.**

That's why it's difficult, if not impossible, to be a great investor if you don't believe in capitalism. If you don't believe in capitalism, then you don't think there's going to be a positive return on the capital you're investing in a company. And if there's no return on capital, capitalism would have failed a long time ago—in the United States as well as in other free market countries.

In a market-based economy, four inputs are typically required for the creation of wealth: One of them is clearly the natural resources that both people and companies need. Another is the skilled labor—the employees and other talented people who are involved in the market. Intellectual capital is a third. The fourth input is financial capital, as when an investor purchases stock or decides to hold bonds.

> **The Four Essential Ingredients of Wealth**
> 1. Natural resources
> 2. Skilled labor
> 3. Good ideas
> 4. Investors

When you're providing capital to corporations, they can create returns, increase their stock prices, pay dividends, or pay the coupons on bonds. When that happens, you're practicing capitalism, working on the assumption that the capital market rate of return will go up.

This is important to remember, because, contrary to common belief, a capital investment is not the same as going to Las Vegas. When you make a capital investment, when you purchase stock, *you own something* and have a claim on future earnings and income. It's not just a piece of paper, nor is it simply a string of letters and numbers on a ticker. You own a claim on real assets. You own a piece of a business.

> **When you invest capital, you purchase partial ownership of a real business.**

A lot of people think this is the same thing as gambling. They think the stock market is rigged. No. Going to Las Vegas is speculation. There's no real income. There are no earnings. There are no dividends. *When you speculate, you're betting that a certain outcome will happen.* But when you invest capital, you purchase partial ownership of a real business with real assets.

# THE NONABUNDANT WAY VERSUS THE ABUNDANT WAY

| THE NONABUNDANT WAY | THE ABUNDANT WAY |
|---|---|
| You think stocks are too risky—no better than gambling in Vegas. | You discover stocks are not risky in the long term, offering a high long-term rate of return that will increase the odds of abundance. |
| You pay attention only to the yield on bonds, ignoring the risks of default. | You understand the role of bonds in an investment plan and choose them carefully. |
| You put most of your money into gold or other alternative investments. | You invest in stocks, rather than speculating in alternative investments. |

# CHAPTER 3

# EVERYBODY TAKES RISKS

*Risk is not knowing what you're doing.*
—Warren Buffett

## A GAME OF RISK

What is the biggest financial risk you can take? Many people, when asked this question, immediately respond that it's losing money in the stock market—without understanding that this isn't even close to the biggest risk that the majority of people take with their money. *The biggest risk, in reality, is that you won't meet your financial goals.*

> The biggest financial risk you face is not achieving your financial goals.

People also make the mistake of thinking that by avoiding making an investment decision, they are avoiding risk. But the truth is that by not making any investment decision, you have in fact made a decision. For example, letting the money you have earmarked for retirement sit in a bank account may seem like a riskless decision, but if your goal is to create a future income source that persists, you are in fact taking on an enormous risk. The interest rate on that bank account, if indeed you are earning interest at all, will not come close to keeping up with inflation. By letting your money sit in a bank account, you risk tremendous loss of purchasing power. More important, you risk having a less abundant future.

---

### FOUR MAIN TYPES OF RISK

1.  Potential loss of principal

2.  Loss of purchasing power

3.  Lack of diversification

4.  Failure to achieve your goals

---

Here's an example from real life: I had a client who sold a company for $3 million back in 2010. Uncertain what to do with the proceeds, the client feared that the market was too risky and wanted to wait until things got more clear. The client decided to keep the money in cash, thinking this essentially a riskless option. But in reality, this client was taking on a great deal of risk—and losing:

- **Lost opportunity.** If my client had put that money to work, there would have been the opportunity for a return on it.

- **Lost money.** My client lost money *every year* by staying in cash. Every year that money wasn't at work outearning inflation, the client lost tremendous purchasing power.

With inflation having run an average 2 percent or so a year since 2010, this client who sold the business actually lost money by earning the bank's paltry interest rate of about 0.50 percent. My client said, "We're not going to take any risk! We're going to stay away from the markets and play it safe," but now that money is worth less than $3 million when factoring in loss of purchasing power—because the client didn't invest it. To this day, it's sitting in a money market account, slowly dwindling.

Hopefully you can see that risk is a very misunderstood concept. If it weren't, I wouldn't have spent so much time on it! Unfortunately, people often don't understand these issues until it's too late.

---

### PRESERVING PURCHASING POWER

Let me shift your paradigm for risk. If your goal is to preserve purchasing power across ten or more years, stocks are much safer than bonds are. For example, US Treasury bills, which are backed by the full faith and credit of the government of the world's strongest and largest economy, provide great certainty in the short-term—yet bondholders pay a steep price for this "certainty" in the form of inflation and very low returns.

---

# NEVER CONFUSE RISK
# AND VOLATILITY

We've talked about how risk is misunderstood, but I want to really bring home the fact that there is no such thing as a "no-risk" or "risk-free" option. It's extremely important to understand that, and accept it, as you make investment plans.

**Volatility and risk are not the same thing; to assume so is a big mistake.**

Another thing that trips people up in investing is thinking that volatility and risk are the same things. Volatility is simply a measure of the amount of fluctuation in your portfolio. Indeed, lowering the volatility of your portfolio likely means that you are reducing your future returns. This is especially true if you are in accumulation mode.

Of course, some investors might need to reduce fluctuations in their portfolio. Figuring out when to do that depends on your stage of investing and what your goals are. When you're accumulating wealth and trying to achieve long-term capital goals, you should invite some volatility in your portfolio. A heavy focus on reducing volatility probably isn't needed until you are in the withdrawal stage or within a few years of it.

Another thing that must be taken into account when deciding how much volatility is acceptable is what you're trying to accomplish with it. What is the money for?

**The big questions: What is the money for, and when do you need it?**

Maybe it's for you and your spouse but also for your kids. Why do you need it? For whom and by when? These questions are key when determining acceptable levels of volatility. Without absolute clarity on those, it's impossible to create the right type of investment plan and understand what the biggest risk is.

For example, when my sister-in-law was 14, her widowed mother started a 529 plan for her to help pay for her college. The "who" was her daughter, my sister-in-law; the "why" was to pay for her daughter's education; the "when" was four to five years. Her investment plan looked very different from that of a 35-year-old who is saving for retirement at 65 and who wants $80,000 a year to live on then. Each must understand what it will take to meet his or her goal, as well as the lump-sum value he or she must invest toward his or her timeline. For my mother-in-law, it was a few years, but a 35-year-old has 30 years until retirement and could easily live until age 90—a 50-year timeline. You must understand these basic elements before you can put together a plan for minimizing your biggest risks and increasing your odds of success.

In the case of my mother-in-law, low volatility was in her best interest: over the short term, stock prices are very uncertain. For her, short-term bonds and other investments that would preserve capital and have some return along the way were the best choice.

Unfortunately, that's not what happened. The broker put her money entirely into technology stocks. This was right around the year 2000, when US stocks were about to crash. Many of those stocks went down by more than 50 percent, and because her money had been placed in a portfolio more designed for a 35-year-old's retirement, she lost a great deal. For her, preserving principal was much more important than maximizing return. In this case, lowering volatility and risk of short-term principal loss should have been emphasized over growth.

> **THE THREE THINGS YOU CAN CONTROL—**
> **AND THE ONE YOU CAN'T**
> ### Controllable
> **Market risk:** You can control how much market risk you take in your portfolio through your asset allocation.
> **Taxes:** You can control taxes through tax-advantaged accounts and by being selective about when you realize capital gains.
> **Fees, expenses, and costs:** You can control your costs by using low-cost and commission-free investments.
> ### Uncontrollable
> **Market returns:** Although we might have an idea about what a particular asset class could do in the future, we have no control over the exact returns in the market.

## RISK AND RETURN

Here's a concept that will immediately make you a better investor: Every day you invest in the capital markets, there's a positive expected return. If that weren't the case, the markets would have failed a long time ago. And risk and return are inversely correlated when it comes to investing.

When stocks are going down, the initial media reaction is generally that "stocks are getting riskier" and that it is suddenly "riskier to invest your money." But actually the opposite is true.

Markets can indeed drop extremely quickly as seen in the 2016 Brexit event. When markets go down, the risk is actually decreasing and the expected future returns are now higher.

In Oklahoma, where I live, oil and gas prices are very, very important to our communities, jobs, and economy. When the oil and gas industry is doing well, the local economy does well. Anyone who follows this industry knows that prices can be extremely volatile. Back in 2014, crude oil prices went down 70 percent from their high and did not start going back up substantially until the beginning of 2016. Risk and return works the same way in this market as it does in stocks (except on a much more extreme basis, with oil and gas prices fluctuating by 10 percent on a daily basis during times of high stress in the industry). Typically, when prices are going up, risk is actually going up instead of going down.

Or look at the 2008–2009 financial crisis, when stocks fell globally by more than 55 percent—a huge drop of the kind that doesn't happen very often. But this set the stage for the massive 2009–2014 market recovery, during which the S&P 500 tripled in value from its March 2009 low of 666. During 2008 and 2009, things were extremely scary, and markets were in turmoil, but every day that market went down, the risk was also going down, even though it didn't feel like it. Unfortunately, a lot of people missed out on this explosive market rally because they were afraid of another crash. Looking back, it is clear that 2008–2009 was actually the best and safest time to invest. But it didn't feel that way at the time.

### BRENT CRUDE OIL PRICES, JANUARY 2014-JANUARY 2016

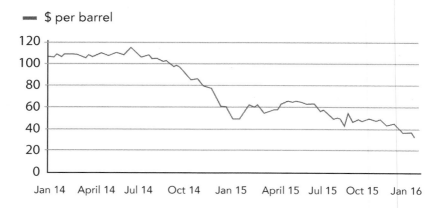

**The Cheerios Law:** When stock prices go down, you should stock up. Let me explain: Stocks are probably the only thing anyone would want to buy simply because they are becoming more expensive. Say you routinely go to the grocery store to buy Cheerios, which typically cost $3.00, and find the price is suddenly $4.50. Would you fill your cart with Cheerios? Of course not. But if you come in one day and those $3.00 Cheerios are on sale for $1.50, then you're going to buy some. It should be the same with stocks: they should be an important part of your investment plan, and if the prices of shares go down, you can take advantage of that and "stock up." If you separate the irrational, emotional, and fearful response you may have in moments of market fluctuation from what you actually do, you stand to benefit.

# FEAR AND FINANCE

Fear is not easy to combat. In fact, it's impossible to completely eliminate fear. I used to think that if I could just get my clients not to feel fear, everything would be great. But now I know that as an advisor, my job, in part, is to help people be more afraid of what might happen if they don't own enough stocks in their portfolio over the long term than of what market fluctuations might do to them in the short term. In short, I make them much *more* fearful—of something that I see as being more dangerous to them.

For example, someone who is 60 years old and close to retiring from his or her job is fearful of the markets crashing in the near term. It's possible, sure, but he or she should be much more afraid of running out of money 30 years from now, than being completely dependent on Social Security or his or her kids. Near-term stock market volatility is scary, but it's more productive to shift that fear away from something that might happen but probably won't to something that happens every day. Volatility might be a source of fear, but we can't let that fear negatively influence our financial decisions.

| DATES OF MARKET PEAK | DATES OF MARKET TROUGH | % RETURN | DURATION | MARKET PEAK | MARKET TROUGH |
|---|---|---|---|---|---|
| 05/29/46 | 06/13/49 | -29.5% | 36.5 mos. | 19.3 | 13.6 |
| 08/02/56 | 10/22/57 | -21.5% | 14.5 mos. | 49.7 | 39.0 |
| 12/12/61 | 06/26/62 | -28.0% | 6.5 mos. | 72.6 | 52.3 |
| 02/09/66 | 10/07/66 | -22.2% | 8.0 mos. | 94.1 | 73.2 |
| 11/29/68 | 05/26/70 | -36.0% | 18.0 mos. | 108.4 | 69.3 |
| 01/11/73 | 10/03/74 | -48.0% | 20.5 mos. | 120.2 | 62.3 |
| 09/21/76 | 03/06/78 | -19.4% | 17.5 mos. | 107.8 | 86.9 |
| 11/28/80 | 08/12/82 | -27.0% | 20.5 mos. | 140.5 | 102.4 |
| 08/25/87 | 12/04/87 | -33.5% | 3.5 mos. | 336.8 | 223.9 |
| 07/16/90 | 10/11/90 | -20.0% | 3.0 mos. | 369.0 | 295.5 |
| 07/17/98 | 08/31/98 | -19.3% | 1.5 mos. | 1186.8 | 957.3 |
| 03/24/00 | 10/09/02 | -49.2% | 30.5 mos. | 1527.5 | 776.7 |
| 10/09/07 | 03/09/09 | -57.0% | 17.0 mos. | 1565.1 | 676.5 |
| 04/29/11 | 10/3/11 | -19.4% | 5.0 mos. | 1363.6 | 1099.2 |

# HOW TO TELL A
# BEAR FROM A BULL

A "bear market" is when stocks go down by 20 percent or more. If the S&P 500 is at 2000 and it goes down to 1600, that's a 20 percent loss—a bear market. You can expect to have a bear market arise, on average, once every five years. If you look at the chart, we've had 14 bear market periods since the end of World War II. Their severity has ranged from drops of 20 percent to drops of almost 60 percent, as in 2008 and 2009. But the important thing is that we've also recovered—every time. What's more, not only have we recovered, but we have also seen markets advance to much higher levels over time.

Part of the price you pay for getting the higher returns possible through stocks is going through these periods. A drop in the market won't destroy your investment plan—but selling at the wrong time will.

How do you know the right time from the wrong time? Remember the Cheerios Law: if you're still in accumulation mode, why would you want to buy

> **A drop in the market won't destroy your investment plan—but selling at the wrong time will.**

something when it is higher in price? As prices go down, potential returns go up, and risk is actually very low. Bear markets are the best time to increase your savings or to find a use for some cash you might otherwise have left to stagnate. Falling prices mean that it's time to take advantage, especially if you are still in accumulation mode. That's the Cheerios Law. It should be as obvious as the law of gravity, yet emotions get the best of people in these decisions, clouding our perspective.

## THE NONABUNDANT WAY
## VERSUS THE ABUNDANT WAY

| THE NONABUNDANT WAY | THE ABUNDANT WAY |
|---|---|
| Falling prices means that risk is increasing in the market. | Falling prices means that risk is decreasing in the market and that potential returns are going up. |
| If I choose to leave my money in cash, there is no risk. | Choosing to do nothing is still a choice, with risks attached. |
| Volatility and risk are exactly the same thing. | Volatility is not synonymous with risk, and some volatility can be good. |

# CHAPTER 4

# AN INVESTOR'S THEORY OF TIME

*Fear has a greater grasp on investors than the*
*impressive weight of historical evidence.*
—Jeremy Siegel, author of *Stocks for the Long Run*

## USING THE MARKET, ABUSE BY THE MARKET

When I'm talking to someone about life and about investing, vision manifests itself in many different ways through my role as advisor. I frequently meet people who have a very difficult time looking into the future or even thinking about their future self. Just as a 30-year-old may have trouble envisioning himself or herself at age 50 or 60, so a 60-year-old will naturally struggle to envision life at 80 or 90. But if that person can learn how to get in the mindset of his or her future self, investing for abundance will be much easier.

People vastly underestimate their timeline. I often hear people say things like, "I'm five years away from retiring, so I plan to get out of most or all of my stocks." The problem is that even if they are five years away from retirement, it's completely possible—even probable—that many of them will live 30 years after the date they retire. According to actuarial studies of a wife and husband who are 62 and don't smoke, the odds are high that at least one of them will still be alive into his or her 90s.

It's easy to lose sight of that reality. We invest for a lifetime, but we experience the market daily. The more you look at your portfolio, the more you might want to trade and tinker and tweak, which means you're probably going to do more damage to your portfolio. Change is a constant in life. The market changes all the time, but how often do your goals change? Probably not often.

> We invest for a lifetime, but we experience the market daily.

When we look at the market every day, it's self-defeating, and it leads to emotional decision making, which is usually bad for your future investment results.

## THE LIFETIME OF THE MARKET

If you follow an investment plan that doesn't look ahead at least ten years, there's a good chance that you're not going to be successful. But if you have the ability to look forward 10, 20, or even 30 years down the road, you're going to have a great advantage over people who are caught up in what's happening in the market today. Think about it for a minute: Do you recall what the market was doing five years ago? How about even a year ago? In the same way, 10 or 20 years from now, you will not remember what you were worried about in the markets today.

In any given year, stocks might be down 30 percent or up well over 50 percent. However, if you are able to look out at least ten years, it's almost a slam dunk that you will have a positive annualized return even over a historically poor ten-year period. Looking out even further over a 20-year period gives even better results. The years that make up each one of those 20 years are uncertain, but the full 20-year period is much more likely to reveal a fairly positive outcome.

## BEST/WORST 1-YEAR RETURNS

### January 1973 - December 2016

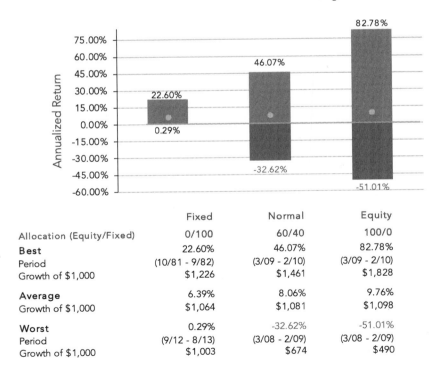

● Average Annualized Return

|  | Fixed | Normal | Equity |
|---|---|---|---|
| Allocation (Equity/Fixed) | 0/100 | 60/40 | 100/0 |
| **Best** | 22.60% | 46.07% | 82.78% |
| Period | (10/81 - 9/82) | (3/09 - 2/10) | (3/09 - 2/10) |
| Growth of $1,000 | $1,226 | $1,461 | $1,828 |
| **Average** | 6.39% | 8.06% | 9.76% |
| Growth of $1,000 | $1,064 | $1,081 | $1,098 |
| **Worst** | 0.29% | -32.62% | -51.01% |
| Period | (9/12 - 8/13) | (3/08 - 2/09) | (3/08 - 2/09) |
| Growth of $1,000 | $1,003 | $674 | $490 |

# BEST WORST 10-YEAR RETURNS

### January 1973 - December 2016

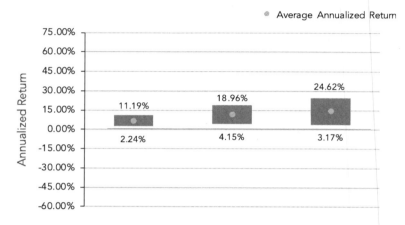

| | Fixed | Normal | Equity |
|---|---|---|---|
| Allocation (Equity/Fixed) | 0/100 | 60/40 | 100/0 |
| **Best** | 11.19% | 18.96% | 24.62% |
| Period | (3/80 - 2/90) | (9/77 - 8/87) | (9/77 - 8/87) |
| Growth of $1,000 | $2,889 | $5,676 | $9,037 |
| **Average** | 6.87% | 11.80% | 14.68% |
| Growth of $1,000 | $1,943 | $3,050 | $3,935 |
| **Worst** | 2.24% | 4.15% | 3.17% |
| Period | (12/06 - 11/16) | (3/99 - 2/09) | (3/99 - 2/09) |
| Growth of $1,000 | $1,248 | $1,501 | $1,367 |

## BEST WORST 20-YEAR RETURNS

January 1973 - December 2016

● Average Annualized Return

|  | Fixed | Normal | Equity |
|---|---|---|---|
| Allocation (Equity/Fixed) | 0/100 | 60/40 | 100/0 |
| **Best** | 9.23% | 16.12% | 20.73% |
| Period | (8/73 - 7/93) | (10/74 - 9/94) | (10/74 - 9/94) |
| Growth of $1,000 | $5,847 | $19,871 | $43,246 |
| **Average** | 6.84% | 11.74% | 14.63% |
| Growth of $1,000 | $3,756 | $9,203 | $15,342 |
| **Worst** | 3.49% | 7.44% | 8.23% |
| Period | (1/97 - 12/16) | (3/96 - 2/16) | (3/89 - 2/09) |
| Growth of $1,000 | $1,986 | $4,199 | $4,860 |

---

## ESTABLISHING A TIMELINE

Your timeline, at its most basic, is this:

Your age + your goals + how long your
money needs to last

Remember the 62-year-old nonsmoking couple we just talked about? They know that they need to make an investment plan that can see them into their 90s.

---

**Don't be shortsighted.** If you're in your 60s and your investment plan is completely focused on maintaining principal, you're not looking far enough into your future. You're underestimating your timeline, and you're overlooking your greatest risk. Although you're distracted by fear of what is happening in the market now, you should really be afraid of what will happen if you outlive your money.

When people begin thinking that way, it's easier for them to feel confident about an investment plan built around stocks. When you're thinking about a longer timeline, you're going to worry less about what happens from year to year and focus more on real concerns—such as whether your money will outperform inflation or keep up with your income needs as you get older.

## YOUR MONEY TODAY WILL LIKELY
## BUY LESS TOMORROW

$0.09 = Quart of milk     $0.09 = 1 small glass of milk    $0.09 = 7 Tablespoons of milk

Within one lifetime, the price of things we purchase, such as milk, postage stamps, and gasoline, has risen tremendously. How many times have these prices risen during the past 20 or 30 years, and by how much? Remember what we said about how long the average 62-year-old nonsmoking couple will likely live? Looking at what postage stamps, milk, and other products cost 30 years ago will give you a good clue of how much they will go up in a retiree's lifetime.

Personally, I am much more frightened at the thought of being dependent on family members or the government in my old age than I am by the prospect of experiencing ups and downs in my portfolio. If you don't want to be a 90-year-old leaning on your children, don't worry about the next 1,000-point move the Dow makes; worry about the next 10,000- or 20,000-point move. History gives us a good idea of the direction of the next 10,000- or 20,000-point move, but no one has any idea in what direction the next 1,000-point move will be—nor does it matter.

People tell me all the time, "I am a conservative investor and do not want to do anything risky. *No risk for me* is the message!"

A financial advisor whom I greatly respect says this when clients make such a comment: "I'm conservative, too, and don't like taking on a lot of risk, which is why I have all stocks, you know? I'd rather have lower risk—because, you see, my timeline is at least 25 years until I retire, and then I need to make sure it lasts." If my friend didn't understand his timeline and didn't have enough stocks, that would be a huge risk indeed.

Jeremy Siegel discusses this concept in his book *Stocks for the Long Run*. In it, he looks at the entire history of the market, plotting its course over 210 years. On average, the real return is 6.5 percent. (Real return, remember, is the return minus inflation.) An average return of 6 to 7 percent is pretty strong if your desire is future abundance. If your goal is to make sure that you never run out of money and that you're able to achieve a return far and above inflation, stocks are the way to go.

# FORWARD THINKING

---

**THE QUESTIONS YOU NEED TO ANSWER BEFORE YOU RETIRE . . .**

Where do you want to live?

Who do you want to be around?

What do you want to be doing with your extra time?

---

When we don't plan with the right timeline in mind, we miss out on a lot of great opportunities. What is your vision for your life? Life in your later years has the potential to be great, but you have to think about it and plan for it. Remember—by failing to plan, you are planning to fail.

One of my favorite questions to ask people is this: "How do you see your life in your 60s, 70s, and 80s?"

Being in your 60s and 70s looks very different now than it did 40 years ago, when I was born. People can do many things in their 70s thanks to advances in medicine and science—things that they usually couldn't do 20 or 30 years ago. Many people in their 70s and even their 80s find fulfillment in nonprofit endeavors or mentoring, in starting new businesses, or in traveling around the world. Partly this is because healthcare has gotten better. When my grandfather was in his 70s, he spent all day in his chair watching television. I don't remember his ever having gotten up, but that's not how things are today.

## LIFE EXPECTANCY - UNITED STATES

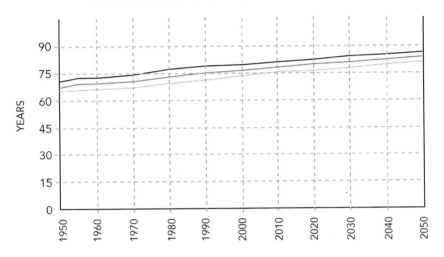

The difference between how my grandparents thought and acted a mere 20 years ago and how the 70-year-olds I meet today think and act is incredible. As far as I can see, this difference isn't going to diminish—instead, it will intensify. People have many more opportunities to make their 70s one of the best decades of their life.

An investment plan is there to enhance that time. It takes the pressure off so that work can be optional. If people do work in their 70s, it's because they want to.

---

**A well-constructed investment plan means that you're not dependent on your family, on Social Security, or on your job—and that if you decide to work, it's not because you have to work!**

---

# THREE WAYS TO USE A TIMELINE

When I meet with clients, we are always very goal-focused. There are a few questions we always come back to while we're talking:

- What is the goal?

- When is the deadline for that goal?

- Are we on track to meet that goal?

One of the ways we use clients' timelines is to measure how we're doing on trying to **meet their goals**. We can measure their progress to see whether we're ahead of schedule or falling behind, and we can use it to determine why. Was it a low-return year for the markets? Did the client not meet his or her savings goals? Is the goal still realistic, or do we need to reevaluate it?

The timeline also serves as a **reality check**. Are you or are you not on track to meet your goal by the deadline you set? I go through clients' plans to see where they are and whether they're being honest with themselves about their goals. If they're way ahead of the game, that's great. But we also need to remain focused on the goal, sticking with our savings and investment plans: not every year is going to be a positive-return year.

If I realize that a client is going to fall short, we discuss his or her options, which typically include increasing contributions, changing the timeline, or seeing how we can adjust the client's investment plan to boost investment returns.

A timeline is a yardstick for measuring your progress. With the help of your trusted advisor, you can build your own timeline, and this alone will put you far ahead of the average investor. You'll be well on your way to achieving abundance with your investment plan.

# THE NONABUNDANT WAY
# VERSUS THE ABUNDANT WAY

| THE NONABUNDANT WAY | THE ABUNDANT WAY |
|---|---|
| See retirement as a one-time event rather than a 30-year ongoing event, causing you to sell most of your stocks. | Realize that you don't need all your money during your first year of retirement; plan to hold stocks during your retirement years. |
| Experience the market daily and allow it to affect your investment decisions. | Ignore the daily market fluctuations, and invest for a long lifetime. |
| Don't worry about a timeline or about measuring your progress toward your goals. | Measure your progress carefully against your timeline each year, adjusting your plan accordingly. |

# CHAPTER 5

# THE SMART INVESTOR'S NEARLY FREE LUNCH: DELICIOUS DIVERSIFICATION

*The only investors who shouldn't diversify are*
*those who are right 100 percent of the time.*
—Sir John Templeton

## DIVERSIFICATION: THE CLOSEST THING TO A FREE LUNCH

Nobel Prize winner and economist Merton Miller once said that diversification is the closest thing to a free lunch, and it's really true. Although diversification isn't a completely free lunch, it is about as close to one as you're going to get. There are many benefits to diversifying your investment plan, and the drawbacks are minimal. Perhaps the biggest drawback to diversification is that you will likely always hate something in your portfolio—the position that is performing the worst.

The great investment writer Nick Murray once said, "Diversification guarantees you will never make a killing, but, more importantly, guarantees that you will never get killed." Short-sightedness is what trips some people up on diversification: they want to be at the top, getting the highest returns every year. What Murray is saying is that when you diversify, you're generally not going to be at the very top of the heap, but you also won't be at the bottom. Over time, diversification will allow you to have great returns—well above most investors out there—because you didn't get killed along the way.

## DON'T CONCENTRATE!

Don't get me wrong, some people have done very well by concentrating instead of diversifying. Some business owners and successful real estate investors concentrate their wealth in one area to become successful. They take on a lot of risk, and sometimes they get rewarded for that risk when it works out for them. Of course, there are many more exceptions to than examples of the rule.

Andrew Carnegie was the opposite of Templeton. He was a successful concentrator of wealth. He actually once said, "Put all your eggs in one basket . . . and watch the basket grow." It worked very well for him, but 99.9 percent of investors will not be the next Andrew Carnegie, who made his money entirely in steel, or John D. Rockefeller, who concentrated his assets in oil and prospered. What's more, even these two business titans had to diversify eventually to protect and preserve their wealth for future generations.

**Employer stock.** A few years ago, I had an executive from a publicly traded company in her 50s come into my office to ask for advice on her retirement and investment plan. After more than 30 years of working extremely hard, she desired to retire within five years to spend more time with her husband and family. She had been very fortunate in that her company stock price had performed extremely well for many years—so well, in fact that she held more than $2 million in this stock, which made up more than two-thirds of her net worth. After I fully understood her goals and situation, I created a long-term plan to divest this stock to get it down to a much smaller percentage of her net worth. To do otherwise was to increase the risk of her not being able to achieve her retirement goals. But change can cause distress. Unfortunately, she balked at my advice and decided to stick to her plan. Her thinking? Familiar stock had done much better recently than a broadly diversified portfolio would have. Later, when we met again, I asked how her stock had done since our last conversation. Regrettably, her stock had gone down by more than 50 percent, whereas a broadly diversified portfolio would have appreciated by well over 30 percent.

**Fannie Mae.** The story of Fannie Mae stock is another good cautionary tale. Fannie Mae was uniquely designed as a quasigovernment enterprise that trades in the public exchanges. It's not a government agency, but it was a government-sponsored enterprise when it was created and a publicly traded stock. In 2001, it was declared by *Money* magazine America's safest stock—in as many words—with the recommendation that "it's as close as you can get to owning an invincible earning machine."

Fannie Mae's stock was at $79.50 on December 2001. But by 2008, the government had essentially taken it over by bailing it out.

Even with that bailout, the stock price dropped from $79.50 to *less than a dollar*. By 2008, a share of Fannie Mae and a dollar would buy you a candy bar.

Maybe you're convinced by now that you should diversify. So how do you effectively diversify your investment plan? There are three important ways:

---

### THREE WAYS YOU CAN DIVERSIFY

**1. Use funds rather than individual securities.** For example, to get exposure to the US market—or any country's market, for that matter—don't invest in a favorite stock such as Apple. Instead, invest in a fund that holds hundreds of securities, offering exposure to Apple and hundreds of other securities as well.

**2. Broadly diversify your assets over global asset classes.** Don't invest only in one type of asset class such as US large company stocks—you also should invest in small company stocks, non-US stocks, and other asset classes.

**3. Use bonds to provide a diversification benefit—** something that helps provide a buffer against market shocks that may arise. Having bonds in your portfolio also prevent you from being forced to sell stocks when they are dropping sharply.

---

# YOU CAN'T SEE THE FUTURE

Fundamentally, diversification is an admission of lack of foresight. I want you to acknowledge that we don't know what's going to happen before lunchtime tomorrow, let alone ten years down the road. No one else knows, either, but the good news is that this doesn't matter when it comes to being successful in investing.

Top investment thinkers, including Warren Buffet and Sir John Templeton, have certainly accepted the fact that we don't know what tomorrow will bring. Buffett is quoted as saying that "forecasts may tell you a great deal about the forecaster, but they tell you nothing about the future."

Not diversifying means accepting the potential for losing everything. It's kind of like the Vegas strategy: "I'm going to Vegas. I've got a certain amount of money, and I hope I do well. But if I don't and I lose it all—which is likely—then I can accept that, and I, understand that ahead of time." When you concentrate, or speculate, you're not really investing: you're playing the slots.

# MUTUAL FUNDS AND ETFS

Both mutual funds and ETFs (exchange-traded funds) should be an important part of your diversification plan. Instead of buying one stock, you're buying into a fund that typically contains hundreds of stocks or securities. This saves you the trouble and expense of buying hundreds of stocks individually.

Both mutual funds and ETFs allow you to gain diversification benefits with one fund. The big difference is that a mutual fund is an "open-ended" fund that trades at the end of each trading day. The point of a mutual fund is that it doesn't trade during the day. There's no difference in buying mutual funds the first thing in the morning or at the end of the trading day. An exchange-traded fund, on the other hand, trades all day long during regular market hours, just like a stock. That means that the price fluctuates during the day. Neither one is necessarily better than the other; both are effective for diversifying.

Literally thousands of funds will provide direct exposure to the US stock space. It's important to diversify into other types of funds, however: foreign developed markets, emerging markets, and bond funds are all good elements in a diversified portfolio.

I like to think of the advantage of funds over stocks in this way: one stock is one pencil and mutual fund is 50 pencils, all bound together with rubber bands. You can snap a pencil in two with one hand, but 50 pencils tied together are almost impossible to break. That's the way I look at mutual funds and single stocks. One stock, or even a couple, can snap in your hand, so to speak, but even if a few stocks or securities in a fund aren't doing well, the overall fund will be fine.

## STAR MANAGERS

Bill Miller was with Legg Mason for a very long time. He was a star manager there, and his case is worth studying. Generally, US fund managers use the S&P 500 as the primary benchmark of their performance. Unbelievably, Bill Miller was able to outperform the S&P 500 index for 15 straight years, which is a record by far. From 1991 to 2005, he managed funds at Legg Mason that performed better than the S&P 500. It's unclear whether this was due more to skill than to luck. Likely, it was a combination of both.

There were other things going on with Bill Miller's funds than record-breaking performance, however. Morningstar, the financial tracking company, showed that the real return for investors during this period was 7.96 percent. While Bill Miller's funds were performing at 11.41 percent, the average investor in his funds had a return that was about 3.5 percent lower than the fund's reported return. How could this be? The reason is simple: investors chase performance, and what fund better to chase performance with than that associated with Mr. Miller's record-breaking performance?

That's not the whole story, though. Eventually, that streak of great performance had to end. Even the brightest star managers have bad runs, and Bill Miller had a truly bad run from 2006 to 2011 after his 15 years of beating the index. His fund lost 7.4 percent, annualized, for the next six years, placing him near the bottom of his benchmark group. To make things even worse, his 2006–2011 performance was so bad that it erased all the gains of his 15-year record-breaking run! This occurred during a period when stock returns as a whole were still positive. Miller went from being one of the best to one of the worst. When you're chasing performance and trying to find a star manager, you're probably going to be late to the game, unable to earn all the return you should. There's also a really good probability that you're going to get in at the point when that manager's luck or skill runs out.

Morningstar is known for evaluating mutual funds and assigning a star rating for funds. Ostensibly, a five-star rating is the best you can have, while one- or two-star ratings are considered suboptimal. The interesting thing here is that multiple studies have shown that five-star funds, after receiving that rating, actually underperform one- and two-star funds. In other words, you're are probably better off picking a one-star fund than a five-star fund. This is a head-scratcher for many, but any approach that is backward-looking is doomed to failure.

## DIVERSIFICATION SMOOTHS OUT SOME OF THE BUMPS

A well-diversified portfolio can provide the opportunity for a more stable outcome than a single security.

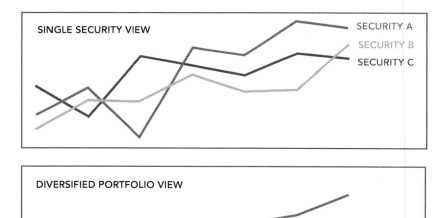

WHAT IS DIVERSIFICATION *NOT?*

Diversification is *not* buying a handful of stocks. Nor is it buying a handful of mutual funds. Even if you bought ten stocks and told yourself, "This is good! I bought ten stocks, instead of one or two!"

that wouldn't make your portfolio diversified. It's very possible that all ten of those stocks will do poorly in a given year, or even over several years, especially if they are in the same industry. This can be where mutual funds come into play, but fundamentally, you need at least 50 different types of stocks or securities to form a diversified fund—and more than 50 is preferable.

But diversification is also more than buying a handful of mutual funds that you saw had five stars on Morning Star. That's something else I see pretty frequently: people who think, "I bought a few mutual funds that were highly rated. They've all done well lately!" That typically means that they're the same kind of mutual fund and that they will likely all go down at the same time!

For example, during the late 1990s, US large-cap growth stocks were shooting out the lights, driven by the technology and internet boom. Many of these stocks were doubling every two or three years. Naturally, US large cap growth mutual funds did quite well at that time and tended toward the top of the performance charts. If you bought six US large-cap growth mutual funds, you basically bought the same one six times: at that time, many of them were composed of telecom and dot-com stocks. When late 1999 and 2000 rolled around, all of them went down significantly with the bursting of the tech bubble—many of them by more than 70 or 80 percent. As a side note, if you lose 50 percent of your money, what percentage return do you need to make to get back to breaking even? The answer may surprise you: you have to earn 100 percent to get back to where you started. Guess what it takes in return to make up for an 80 percent loss? Would you believe 500 percent?

I got into the financial advice business in 2002. I came across countless clients in the early 2000s who had become very distraught by the time I got to them. Their portfolios were composed almost entirely of technology stocks, and they had lost a significant amount of their retirement plans. A lot of these people were also in their 50s or older, meaning that they were often in a pretty bad place before coming to me with limited earning years ahead. They got badly hurt by thinking they were diversifying by buying a few mutual funds and then realizing that they had gotten the same thing several times in the form of US large cap growth stock funds that had all gone down significantly and wrecked retirement plans. Don't let this happen to you.

Buying a mutual fund or an exchange-traded fund as opposed to an individual security is a good thing, but not even close to being enough. You have to make sure the funds you buy all have different exposures across these global asset classes.

---

### SIX MAJOR ASSET CLASSES TO SEEK OUT

- US large-cap stocks
- US small-cap stocks
- Foreign developed stocks
- Emerging markets stocks
- Real estate investment trusts
- Short-term high-quality bonds

---

## THERE IS NO CRYSTAL BALL

Diversification can't do everything. It doesn't mean that you're going to avoid all short-term volatility. If, for example, the US or even the global markets take a hit, having a diversified portfolio doesn't mean that your portfolio comes out unscathed. It's not a bulletproof deal, especially in the short term. But clearly, broad global diversification is a critical part of a long-term plan and will help to avoid long-term underperformance.

When you diversify, it allows you to plan for a wide range of outcomes. We don't know which asset class will do better than the others. We don't know how the US markets will do against non-US markets; we don't know what inflation will do or what kinds of geopolitical struggles will arise.

## INVEST LIKE AN ALL-STAR

I like to use sports analogies to help me explain investing. For example, when you're diversifying, you're making yourself the kind of hitter who doesn't swing for the fences every time. You're not trying to hit every single ball out of the park because the best hitters don't do that. When you diversify, you're going to be the consistent hitter who's usually near the top of the league in batting percentages. You're trying to hit singles and doubles, shooting for a home run only if the opportunity is there. Sometimes you will hit that home run—scoring that major return—but, more important, you're going to win in the long term and avoid a bunch of strikeouts.

I grew up playing baseball and was a fan of the major leagues. Watching baseball in the 1980s and 1990s, Tony Gwynn, one of the best hitters in the long history of baseball, was one of my heroes. His career batting average was .338, which is absurdly high by historical standards. Tony Gwynn also had more than 3,000 hits. He was a 15-time all-star. Over the course of his 20-season career, he won eight batting titles and never hit below .309 in any given season.

He hit only 135 home runs in his career—a relatively low figure for 20 seasons. But, more important, he very rarely struck out, and by taking the approach to batting that he did, he helped his team, the San Diego Padres, win many games. That's the kind of investing we want to do: not trying to make every at-bat a home run but rather maintaining high overall quality in the long run. Be patient and help your investment team, and you're going to win a lot of games over a long period and be known as a top investor.

## CAUTIONS AGAINST CONCENTRATION

## BURNED ON A HOT STOCK TIP

A doctor client of mine once referred me to one of his partners, who wanted some help with an investment retirement plan. This doctor was in his late 40s, and when we sat down together, he revealed to me that he had put his entire investment account into a single pharmaceutical stock, and not a well-known one either. Even putting all his money into a well-known pharmaceutical stock such as Merck or Pfizer would have been extremely dangerous, but this was suicidal.

As I went through my usual financial planning questions, discussing our investment philosophy of broad global diversification, he said that he felt that his current approach of investing his entire retirement account in one small pharmaceutical company was the best possible strategy. So, ultimately, he put all his retirement savings into one stock, amounting to about $800,000. This was his entire nest egg. Sadly, but not unsurprisingly to me, the stock ended up going all the way to zero. This hardworking doctor had saved $800,000, but he had gotten a hot tip. That Vegas mentality that we talked about earlier took over: "Why would I take a 10 percent return on my money when in this one stock I could get 100 percent this year?" It's seductive, and even otherwise smart and hardworking people fall for it all the time.

If you want to put some money in a hot stock tip, that's fine if it's a small amount of money that you won't miss. You just have to understand that you're speculating—and that you should never do it with money that you're counting on for your investment plan. Otherwise, don't do it. This doctor, unfortunately, got caught up in the emotion, and didn't limit his investment amount, and succumbed to the allure of doubling his money in a short amount of time. Instead, he lost everything.

## THE LOST DECADE

Don't ever let anyone tell you that you should invest only in the United States. Investors call the 2000s "the lost decade" because from 2000 to 2009, the S&P 500—the main US benchmark—actually lost money:

## THE LOST DECADE?

Monthly growth of wealth: January 2000 - December 2009

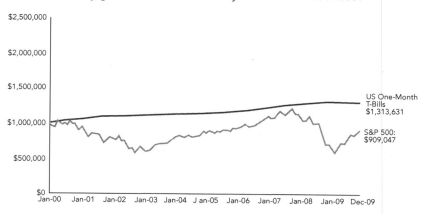

If you had had all your money in the US large-cap market during that decade, even if you held many different stocks across that market, you would have lost money over the course of this decade that profit forgot. The S&P 500 is, essentially, the US large-cap market, and if that's where all your money had been during that period, whether in individual securities or in mutual funds, you'd have lost badly. That's why it's so important to diversify into different asset classes and different markets.

### Home Market Index Portfolio

S&P 500
1 country, 500 stocks

### Global Market Index Portfolio

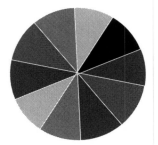

MSCI All County World Index (IMI)
46 countries, 8,716 stocks

## A LOOK BEYOND LARGE CAP
## DEVELOPED EQUITY MARKETS

Monthly growth of wealth: January 2000 - December 2009

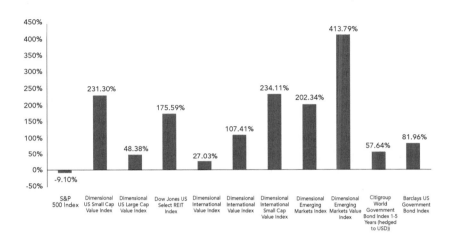

## A DIFFERENT EXPERIENCE

Monthly growth of wealth: January 2000 - December 2009

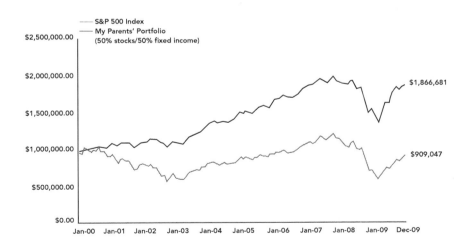

If someone had decided "Hey! I'm only going to invest in the United States, because the rest of the world is dangerous" and then left his or her money in the S&P 500 for the ten-year period ending in 2010, that person would have been in a bad place. In dollar terms, had you invested $1 million in the S&P 500 on January 2000, you would have had less than $900,000 by the end of 2009. Had you been in retirement and making withdrawals during this period, your portfolio would have been decimated.

## A GLOBAL CONCERN

Concentrating on one particular global market is not a US-only mistake. It can happen in any country to any investor. It's typically most dangerous for the citizens of that country: US citizens tend to be biased toward US stocks, much as Japanese citizens can be biased toward Japanese stocks or Europeans towards European stocks. Japan went through its own lost decade ten years before the US. The country had become a dominant force back in the 1980s, when its economic and stock growth were crushing growth in the United States. At this time, Japan was becoming a dominant force in electronics and automobiles. The Nikkei Index, Japan's major market exchange, outperformed US stocks by more than 200 percent throughout the 1980s. Had you been a Japanese-only investor during this time, as many Japanese citizens were, you might have said, "Why would I invest anywhere else?" Because Japan was such a power in the world economy and markets, Japanese real estate investors began buying up some of the most valuable property in the United States, including the Rockefeller Center and more than $50 billion worth of US real estate.

But when the 1990s rolled around, the tables turned. The US market easily outperformed the Japanese one throughout the 1990s, and the majority of those massive US real estate purchases made by the Japanese were quickly sold back to US real estate investors, often at massive losses in bankruptcy court. Japan has yet to recover.

## NIKKEI STOCK INDEX

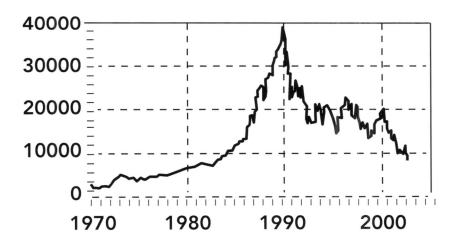

# THE NONABUNDANT WAY
# VERSUS THE ABUNDANT WAY

| THE NONABUNDANT WAY | THE ABUNDANT WAY |
|---|---|
| Use a crystal ball approach, trying to pick the "hot" stocks. | Embrace your inability to see the future, then construct a plan that doesn't require you to. |
| Tactically buy several of the same type of fund, or buy only funds that have performed well recently (the Morningstar five-star fund approach). | Strategically buy funds that avoid overlap times by buying multiple asset class funds. |
| Don't diversify outside the US, thinking it too risky and likely to reduce your returns. | Invest across global markets to reduce your risk and increase your returns. |

# CHAPTER 6

# THE WELL-TIMED PAUSE: OFTEN THE BEST THING TO DO IS . . . NOTHING

*Don't do something; just stand there!*
–Jack Bogle, founder of the Vanguard Group

Warren Buffett, widely considered the greatest investor of all time, often quoted his mentor Ben Graham when the 1990s rolled around: "In the short run, the market is a voting machine. In the long run, it is a weighing machine."

During the decade when Buffett was saying this, his Berkshire Hathaway stock was languishing relative to most of the markets as tech stocks were going through the roof. To put this in perspective, from 1995 to 1999, a $100,000 investment in the flagship technology company of the time, Microsoft, would have grown to more than $1.5 million, whereas a $100,000 investment in Berkshire Hathaway would have grown to "only" $275,000. But Buffett wasn't worried about the short run because those prices weren't based on what's real. In the short term, prices go up based on popularity and what is trending. This is a great reminder that if you're invested right, you probably don't need to react, even when it seems like everyone around you is reacting.

Let's be clear: Successful investing is not meant to be a very exciting thing. Despite how it seems on CNBC, successful investing is not particularly fast-paced or sexy. It isn't something you track on a day-to-day basis. The most successful investors take a very boring, long-term approach compared to a typical Wall Street approach. Ultimately, this should be liberating: if you have the right investment plan, you don't have to check on it all the time. And most of the time, the best thing to do is nothing. Boring is good when it comes to investing.

Remember: If your goals haven't changed, then you probably don't need to do anything. It doesn't really matter what the market's doing right now. All that matters is what happens throughout the course of your investment timeframe, which should be longer than this month, this year, or even the next five years.

> **Most of the time, the best thing to do is nothing. Boring is good when it comes to investing.**

It is hard to "just stand there." It doesn't feel right, and it feels like you're being lazy. But in investing, after you've done your research, being lazy is a good thing. Warren Buffett talks about that all the time: Be lazy. Take time to read. Don't spend too much time messing with things. If history is any guide, you'll do better in the long run.

---

### DOING BETTER BY DOING NOTHING

- Investing shouldn't be exciting.

- If your goals haven't changed, you probably don't need to do anything.

- Embrace being lazy when it comes to investing.

---

This is not to say that it's never necessary to take action. There are times when you should. The key is to make sure that you're taking *needed* action, rather than just *reacting* to a market event. Successful investors are always proactive. Instead of acting on a market trend, or a news story, they ignore this garbage and only act according to their plan.

## A DANGEROUS DISTRACTION: POLITICAL AND ECONOMIC FORTUNE-TELLING

One of the more fundamental things about successful investing is to understand that media entities are not your friends. I like to joke with people, "Think about this: what if CNBC and *Money* magazine and all other financial media decided to tell people every single day to make sure they have a strong investment plan and to focus on the long term?" It's sound investing, but it's really bad entertainment. They'd all be out of business in a week.

Never forget, media entities are there primarily to grab your attention. They will do whatever it takes to get it. Paying too much attention to the media is a very expensive distraction.

Whenever the media get into political or economic fortune-telling, it's very clear, historically, that they're not a consistent forecaster. Economic forecasts don't improve your returns—in fact, they typically do the opposite. Peter Lynch, arguably the most successful fund manager of all time, once famously said, "Far more money has been lost by investors preparing for corrections than has been lost in corrections themselves." By trying to *guess* when the market will go down, you risk losing out on the abundance that comes by ignoring forecasts and being invested when it inevitably goes back up.

## PATIENCE

Exercising the kind of patience we've been talking about in this chapter is always a challenge. Indeed, it's probably the most difficult part of investing for people to master. I think this is especially hard for US citizens. We're not patient, and we always want to be striving for something or doing something.

# THREE TIMES TO MAKE CHANGES

All that said, sometimes you do need to make some changes. There are three main times when this will happen:

1.  If you experience changes to your financial goals or life situation, such as a business sale or retirement.

2.  If one of your portfolio's positions gets significantly overweighted or underweighted.

3.  If your portfolio volatility is keeping you awake at night.

A change in goals or aspirations is common and is nothing to stress over. I like to tell clients that you always have the right to change your specific goals in the future: nothing is set in stone. For example, if you get married, lose your job, or sell your business, your situation is different, and your goals might well change. When you started out, your goal was to retire at 60 with $100,000 a year. But a few years down the road, you may change your mind, and say, "I actually love my job, and I don't want to retire until I have to. Let's push that retirement back to 65 or even later." We may want to change your asset allocation or make some changes in your savings plan to take that into account. This is all about being proactive with your planning and making the necessary adjustments to ensure that your portfolio is still aligned with your own best interests.

Sometimes markets do go through long periods of time when certain asset classes—US stocks, or emerging markets, for example—make an extreme move up or down. That's an opportunity to rebalance your portfolio to take that into account. This is a proactive move that is completely based on predetermined levels: it's not trying to time the markets or anything like that. The decision to rebalance your portfolio should be triggered by predetermined percentages of performance based on your timeline, not a kneejerk emotional reaction to the markets. For example, in 2008 and 2009, all stocks were way down. Most people thought, "Oh, I need to get out of stocks, because they are too risky and will go down more!" That would actually have been the worst time to sell stocks. If anything, this should have been a clear sign to buy stocks. Remember when we talked about buying things on sale? It seems counterintuitive, but that's what rebalancing does for you. More on this later.

It's a lot better to just bite the bullet and stick with your plan than it is to try to analyze every little blip on the market radar. Sometimes people really can't handle what's happening in the market on a daily basis and need to adjust their plan. That's when we might want to consider reducing the volatility in their portfolio. After all, if you're losing sleep over the state of the marketplace, you might want to consider owning a portfolio that you can stick with through turbulence. A strong stomach is more useful than a strong mind when it comes to investing.

## SURFING CORRECTIONS

When you're surfing, you need to let the waves work for you rather than trying to time them or, worse, work against them. You might get lucky every once in a while, but you're going to wipe out much more often if you don't follow the appropriate steps, and waiting for the waves to take you where you want to go. The same is true of the markets. Instead of trying to time them or predict them, it's much better to let them carry you both up and down but trending up over time. You're going to be in a much stronger position with your investments.

---

### THREE WAYS TO INVEST LIKE A SURFER

- Don't look at your account every day: quarterly is more than enough. Annually is even better.

- Ignore the short-term market trends and the media when it comes to investment intel. It's a waste of time—and it will stress you out.

- Find your excitement outside of your investments. Remember, you're investing so that you can do exciting things. If investing is exciting for you, you're likely to wipe out—quickly.

---

If you need to make investing more exciting, open a small account—a separate account from your long-term investment account. Bring only as much money there as you can afford to lose because you're probably going to lose. But if investing is fun for you, budget for it the way you would for entertainment. It's not part of your long-term strategy; it's just for fun and shouldn't be counted toward your retirement goals. Never use your retirement money; keep it separate. You don't want to wipe out!

# THE NONABUNDANT WAY VERSUS THE ABUNDANT WAY

| THE NONABUNDANT WAY | THE ABUNDANT WAY |
|---|---|
| Look at your account every day, letting it affect your daily mood. | Review your account no more than quarterly. Annually is even better. |
| Analyze market forecasts, making frequent trades and constantly tinkering with your portfolio. | Ignore all market forecasts, making changes to your portfolio only when your plan dictates. |
| See investing as exciting. Try to time the market. | Make your investment plan boring so that you can do exciting things with the money you earn. |

# CHAPTER 7

# THE ENEMIES
# WITHIN

*The investor's chief problem, and even his*
*worst enemy, is often himself.*
—Sir John Templeton

Jim Collins, in his classic business book *Good to Great*, talks about how every successful company needs to have a "stop doing" list. This list, he says, is even more important than a "to do" list. If you know what not to do, it's a lot easier to focus your efforts on the things that will help you succeed. In that same spirit, you need to be able to recognize the enemies of your success.

# THE ENEMIES OF YOUR SUCCESS—A BAKER'S DOZEN

## 1. YOU

A couple years ago, we were sitting down with one of our best clients to try to get feedback. We asked, "What do you value most about our firm?" We wanted to make sure we were doing more of the things our clients value, not the things they don't need us to do.

After a minute, the client said, "Kendall, I think the thing that's most valuable about what you do for me and my family is that you just help me get out of my own way." Often, he explained, he understood what we were doing and why we were doing it. But he knew that on his own, he would get in his own way, tripping himself up. In general, this is the biggest problem people have: they're their own worst enemy.

## 2. UNDERESTIMATING LIFE EXPECTANCY

As people, we tend to underestimate how long we will live. We've talked about this before, and it's something you need to plan for. I've seen a lot of smart people underestimate how long they're going to live, and it can really hurt them because they are investing to live into their 70s rather than their 90s. Remember the milk illustration: plan on the things you buy doubling in price over a 30-year retirement.

# 3. HUMAN BIASES

We all have a few very common biases that affect us every day, frequently affecting our decision making, including when investing. It's crucial to understand these so that you can reduce their negative effects on your returns. The five types I see most often are:

- Overconfidence

- Recency bias

- Hindsight

- Confirmation bias

- Loss aversion

Let's look at each one.

**Overconfidence**. Put 100 people in a room and ask above-average drivers to raise their hands, and you're going to have something like 80 or 90 hands in the air. In general, we tend to have too much confidence in our abilities. This happens in the investment world all the time: people get very overconfident in their investment skills, particularly if they occasionally get lucky and pick a stock that does well.

In the late 1990s, pretty much all tech stocks, and especially internet stocks, were going through the roof. People routinely made returns of 50 to 100 percent in a very short amount of time. Those kinds of profits caused many people to fall prey to the overconfidence bias, with people jumping on the bandwagon and blindly picking tech stocks, convinced that they would continue to do well. A lot of people abandoned their more middle-of-the-road investment plans in the hope of striking gold. Sadly, this approach wrecked many of these investors' retirement plans when the tech bubble popped in 2000.

We all have this kind of overconfidence in some area of our lives, and it can be very harmful if you don't recognize it.

**Recency bias** is another common problem I encounter. For example, we saw a massive market rally begin in March 2009 when stocks started going back up again. Still, everyone seemed to fear that the markets would go down again right away. This fear caused many people to sit on too much cash for far too long, rather than sticking with their investment plans. Then the market went up by about 200 percent between 2009 and 2013, and a lot of people missed out on that growth. Major events, such as the crash in 2008, typically happen about once every 30 or 40 years. And the odds of our having dramatic events such as these are actually much lower if one happened recently. It's the opposite of what we think will happen, but as humans, we can't help but feel as we do.

> Major events, such as the crash in 2008, typically happen about once every 30 or 40 years.

A noninvestment example of recency bias is seen in the effect 9/11 had on the travel industry. For 12 months after that tragedy, no one wanted to fly—so that same period saw almost 1,600 more deaths than would have been predicted statistically. Instead of flying, people were driving, forgetting that you're a lot more likely to die on any given car trip than on any given plane ride. People, falling victim to this recency bias, were traveling by car instead of by plane because this recent event loomed so large for them—and it took its toll.

**Hindsight** on the surface may seem similar to recency, but it's actually a little different. Do you know a Monday morning quarterback? Or perhaps you are one yourself! This is the guy who, on Monday morning, replays alternate versions of the football game: "*If* we had just done this, we could have won! *If* the coach had only played this guy instead, or if he had thrown the ball more, the game would have gone our way." It's easy to say those things with the benefit of hindsight. Hindsight tricks us into thinking we knew something but simply failed to act on it. Looking back always offers 20/20 vision, and it can be very tempting to think you *just* missed it.

This is a dangerous illusion to which we all risk falling prey. Things always seem clear when they have already happened, but almost every time, it's not that you missed the signs—it's that you didn't have all the information you have now. Getting too hung up on thinking of what could have been can greatly hinder your long-term investing strategy by making you afraid to take the actions necessary to move forward with your plan.

**Confirmation bias** is all around us. When you already have a belief system in place, even if it's flat-out wrong, you unconsciously seek out things that will support that belief system. Whether it's a 55-year-old telling me that he shouldn't invest in stocks because of his age, or whether it's played out in politics by talking heads on television, many people want to hear only things that will support the way they already think.

That's dangerous when it comes to investing. If you're seeking only information that supports your way of thinking, you're not going be able to take appropriate actions. For example, if you are convinced that stocks are going down in the next 12 months, it's likely that you will be attracted to reports that support this thinking.

This may cause you to make a bad decision that negatively affects your future returns. The best investors are very good at putting their biases aside and looking at resources that may conflict with their way of thinking.

**Loss aversion** is another powerful bias—probably the most dangerous one. Bill Russell, the great Celtics player, and himself also eventually a coach, is widely considered the greatest winner in sports history. His legendary Celtics won 11 championships during his time with them, yet he admits that he is still tormented by the two times he didn't win. Those two losses give him more pain than his 11 wins give him pleasure! In finance too, loss causes more emotion than gain does.

Behavioral economists have shown, time and again, that when you lose money, the ensuing pain far outweighs the pleasure you feel when you gain the same amount of money. If you have $100,000 and in the short term your investments go down $20,000, the bad feeling you have when you lose that $20,000 is roughly as intense as the feeling of gaining $40,000. Said another way, a $20,000 loss hurts a lot more than a $20,000 gain feels good. The avoidance of pain is much more of a money motivator than our desire for gain is. Most important, it can prevent you from achieving your goals on your desired timeline.

# 4. MEDIA

The next enemy of our success comes in the form of the media. Fundamentally, the media just want to get your attention and entertain. They're not great when it comes to investing. As Nick Murray says, "Going to the media for investment advice is like going to Sweeney Todd for a haircut." Sometimes clients come in worried about something on the news, but I remind them of CNBC's Jim Cramer and his track record of investment recommendations. He's very entertaining, but—said kindly—his investment track record is very poor compared to a basic low-cost index fund.

It's difficult, if not impossible, to ignore the media, so it's important to take time to think about why we shouldn't listen to them. Never before has there been a greater competition for your attention, and to get it, many in the media will resort to shock value and fearmongering.

Think of your media consumption the same way you think of your food consumption: whatever you take in is going to affect you. The media you consume forms a diet. Just as your diet of food affects your health and your body, if you are constantly reading and watching and listening to investment junk, you're not going to be in good shape. It's just going to distract you and warp your perspective. Unless you find it entertaining, you have my permission to stop watching the news.

## 5. IMPATIENCE

Successful investing requires patience.

Remember Warren Buffett's remark? "My favorite holding period is forever." You can't go into investing thinking that you have to make money now—or even this year. You have to go into it with the knowledge that it's the best thing for your investment plan, working on the assumption that the holdings you now have you might have forever.

We live in an impatient society. Patience, however, is crucial to successful investing. You can do everything right and still screw up by getting antsy if that causes you to make unnecessary changes that will likely be harmful to your perfect investment plan. But, as we discussed in a previous chapter, the best thing to do is . . . nothing.

# 6. EMOTIONS

Emotional decision-making is often the source of investing mistakes. It happens to the best of us: we're all naturally emotional people. Most decisions are made on an emotional level. Many people *think* that they only make decisions rationally, so understanding that you do make emotional decisions, that you can be your worst enemy, and that your emotions can be devastating if you let them drive your decision making is supremely important. I always say, "It's okay to feel that way. There's nothing wrong with the fear or the emotion that you have right now, but that doesn't mean it's okay to act on it." How you feel should not dictate how you invest. Emotions change a lot, especially when things are rough.

A client of mine had $1,000,000. He started investing this money in 2007, went through the financial crisis, saw his $1,000,000 quickly diminish to $600,000 at the beginning of 2009, got very emotional about it, and bailed on the market around the bottom of the downturn—and then the market happened to go up 200 percent between 2009 and 2013. He missed out on something like $1.8 million or greater in less than five years, just because emotions got the best of him. There was no rational reason for him to do it. He made a purely emotional decision, and those can be very harmful to people. I know of dozens of such stories from talking to other advisors.

# 7. HERD MENTALITY

When we decide to do what we see the majority of others in our circle doing, we're sharing a herd mentality. Unfortunately, most people who invest are not doing so correctly. (That's part of why I get up every day.) Often, they got onto that incorrect path by following others. Sometimes, unfortunately, they're following a lemming.

Herd mentality is especially dangerous when the markets go through manias, like what was seen in the late 1990s with the technology bubble: *everyone* jumped in on that and then got hurt really badly. There are countless stories of people who lost 70, 80, or even 90 percent of their money because they were told that technology stocks, especially dot-com stocks, would keep going up.

> **Regardless of what the market's doing, follow your plan, not the herd.**

The same thing happened in the other direction, during the 2008 financial crisis, when people rushed to sell all their stocks. As we discussed earlier, 2008 was the very worst time to sell stocks. Regardless of what the market is doing, follow your plan and listen to your advisor, not the herd.

# 8. NEIGHBOR ENVY

The concept of neighbor envy—what the Bible refers to as covetousness—can be very similar to herd mentality, but there are a few key differences. Rather than doing the same thing as everyone else, you enter into a competition with your neighbors—but trying to keep up with the Joneses can be very dangerous to your success as an investor.

The Joneses may be following their own plan, one that has nothing at all to do with you. Investing is so personal that one of the most dangerous things you can do is take your neighbors' successes personally. When you hear of certain people making returns that sound incredibly good—maybe even too good to be true—it naturally creates a little bit of greed in you. You start comparing yourself to your neighbors, competing with them to get what they have—even though what they have may not be what you need. If you're not completely focused on what's best for your plan and let other people's achievements dictate what you're doing, you risk falling into a spiral of desire, spite, and poor decision making.

## 9. SPECULATING

I often have clients or friends come to me when they've heard about a great stock idea from a really smart person or an "insider." This is speculation, not investing.

When clients come to me with the latest can't-miss tip, I have to tell them, "Remember, speculating is not investing; it's spinning a roulette wheel." Things get dangerous when you start speculating with money you're counting on to meet your long-term goals and retirement income needs.

## MARKETS HAVE REWARDED DISCILPLINE

Growth of a dollar–MSCI World Index (net dividends). 1970-2016

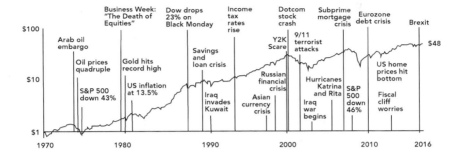

A disciplined investor looks beyond the concerns of today
to the long-term growth potential of markets.

## THE GRAVITY OF 13,000 POUNDS

Isaac Newton was, arguably, one of the smartest people ever to have lived. He was an incredible physicist with a wildly inventive mind. But even his brilliant mind didn't make him a smart investor. As Warren Buffett is famous for commenting, "temperament is more important than IQ when it comes to investing". Newton owned shares in the South Sea Company, which in the 1720s was the hottest stock in England. It was the 1700s equivalent of the 1990s tech and internet boom. And for a while during the 18th century, those stocks were acting in basically the same way as the internet and tech stocks at the end of the 20th century. At first Newton played it right: he sold out after making a 100 percent return on his first investment. But the stock kept rising after he sold, so he decided to buy back in, this time to the tune of £20,000. Perhaps inevitably, the stock crashed, and he sold it again. He ended up losing about £13,000—roughly $2 million in today's dollars. Ouch—that's a heavy loss.

## 10. "HIGH INCOME" PRODUCTS

"High income," also known as "high yield," refers to a class of investment products that focus on generating a high amount of income. Whether a stock, a fund, a convertible bond, or something else, the yield tends to be abnormally higher than other available options. Investors see the yield and think that it's great—and, on the surface, why wouldn't they? The problem arises when people confuse "high yield" with "low risk," whereas it's the other way around. If you have a higher yield, you're likely taking on more risk than you realize. I have a longtime friend who is always bragging about the 8 percent yield on a stock he has owned for years. One day I happened to look at how this particular stock had performed overall in recent years. It wasn't pretty! He was indeed collecting impressive 8 percent dividends each year, but the stock price had gone down by over 20 percent annually for many years, more than offsetting his handsome dividend checks!

Just because a particular stock pays a great dividend doesn't mean that it's automatically a great investment. Apple stock is a great example of what I'm talking about here. For years, Apple (portfolio 1 in the chart below) didn't pay a dividend yield, yet its stock in the 2000s, under Steve Jobs, went through the roof. From 1997 through 2009, a $100,000 investment in Apple, which paid zero dividends during this time, would have grown to over $4 million. Even more, a $100,000 investment in AT&T (portfolio 2, below), which has always paid one of the highest dividends, would not even have doubled its value, despite having paid more than $75,000 of dividends along the way.

## PORTFOLIO GROWTH

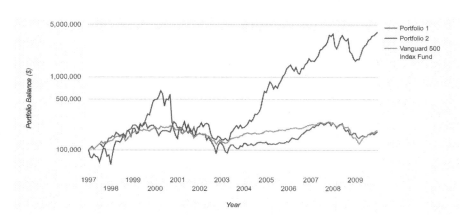

More recently, Apple has actually started paying a dividend yield, and since doing so, it has actually performed worse than during its no-dividend years. This is just one example of why high yield doesn't necessarily mean higher return or lower risk.

## 11. LIFE INSURANCE

As a rule, life insurance is a poor investment tool. Life insurance was originally designed to pay out a death benefit to surviving family members when a death occurred, thereby making sure that they could survive without the income lost by the death of their provider. At some point, insurance companies made life insurance a lot more complex and started adding an investment component to it. These products are referred to as "permanent life insurance" and known by terms such "whole-life insurance," "universal life insurance," or "variable life insurance." Although some of these insurance policies can be helpful in tax and estate planning, they tend to have very overinflated promises, low returns, and high expenses, and they're complex. It's best practice to separate your insurance from your investing unless there are tax or estate planning reasons.

> **It's best practice to separate your insurance from your investing unless there are tax or estate planning reasons.**

## 12. ANNUITIES

Annuities, another insurance-based investment, are a great moneymaker—for the broker selling them and the company issuing them, that is. Unfortunately, they tend to be very poor investments whose "guarantees" are nothing like what they promise. I see them more as a guarantee that you will make very little return—and that you will feed the broker's family.

The main problems with annuities are that they're extremely expensive and not liquid. They typically pay the salesman commissions of 6, 7, or 8 percent—or more. If you put, say, $300,000 into one, it's going to pay the broker somewhere in the neighborhood of $18,000 to $24,000 commission. They also never perform as advertised, and they come up with heavy surrender charges if you want to get out before the first seven to ten years. Their main selling point is that they at least have some guarantees, but those guarantees are not very good—and, what's more, they are only as good as the company. If the company fails, the guarantees go away. I could go on and on about why you should avoid them at all costs, but I hope you get the point already.

# 13. FEAR

Clients often come to me with concerns, worried about politics, that day's big news headline, or the economy. Fear and worry are inevitable: you're always going to have something to be concerned about. But it's going to pass, and then you'll have different fears and different worries. Regardless, you can't let them hinder your investment plan. Legendary fund manager, Peter Lynch once said, "The real key to making money in stocks is not to get scared out of them." We get scared and let our fear cause a bad decision, not thinking things through—and then we make emotional decisions that can be harmful.

As long as we stay away from some of the garbage products just mentioned and stay aware of the enemies of our success, we will find a path to abundance.

## THE NONABUNDANT WAY VERSUS THE ABUNDANT WAY

| THE NONABUNDANT WAY | THE ABUNDANT WAY |
|---|---|
| Allow your biases to affect your investment decisions. | Understand your biases, then develop a plan to overcome them. |
| Look to the media for guidance in your investments. | Ignore the media's investment advice, watching the media only for entertainment. |
| Lean on your emotions for your investment decision, focusing only on the present. | Have a longer-term perspective. Think about investing on a timescale of no less than ten years rather than worrying about what's happening in the short term. |

# CHAPTER 8

# YOUR SECRET WEAPON: YOUR ADVISOR

*I think you're not human if you don't have doubts and fears.*
—Coach Mike Krzyzewski

What an advisor does for you is really a lot like what a coach does for an athlete, in the sense that your potential as an investor will never be reached without the guidance of a coach. A great coach will help you play a longer, stronger game and will eventually guide you to success. That's what I strive to do as an advisor.

I'm a huge college basketball fan and have been for years. If you have any familiarity with the sport, you know that the Duke Blue Devils are a powerhouse. But that wasn't always the case. One of my favorite basketball memories is when Duke was a major underdog in the 1990–1991 Final Four. Coming from a crushing defeat to the UNLV Runnin' Rebels in the championship game of the 1989–1990 season, they had a secret weapon on their side: their coach, Mike Krzyzewski.

It didn't look good for the Blue Devils when the following season they came up against UNLV again—a team that seemed unbeatable and was talked about as perhaps the best team in college basketball history. UNLV had won the national championship the year before and had almost its entire championship team back for 1990–1991, including future NBA players Larry Johnson, Stacey Augmon, and Greg Anthony. The Runnin' Rebels were undefeated going into the Final Four and had won every game that season by double digits. On top of that, they had beaten Duke by about 30 points in the championship game the year before. When they clashed again in the Final Four in 1991, no one gave Duke a fighting chance. UNLV looked as if it couldn't be beaten, and on paper, it was the better team by far.

In this classic underdog story, however, Duke won the game, in large part because of Coach K's coaching style and what he was able to teach these young athletes. The Duke players must have been feeling a lot of doubts and fears before that game, and the 30-point loss the previous year must have been deeply rooted in the backs of their minds. But Coach K was able to instill confidence into the team, helping them feel as if they would win, while also devising some excellent strategies to help them win the game. They pulled the upset off. Coach K helped his players deal with fear and uncertainty, much like an advisor does for frightened investors in uncertain markets.

Defeating UNLV was a monumental victory. And then, two nights later, Duke came up against the University of Kansas. That game needed a different strategy. Against UNLV, Coach K had to get them believing that they actually belonged on the court at all, then get them believing that they could win. Against Kansas, he had to bring them down some. Like investors who get overconfident and perhaps even a little greedy, in a booming bull market, the Duke players probably felt themselves unbeatable.

Sometimes after an upheaval in the markets, people need the belief that they're going to get through it. I saw this a lot after the financial crisis in 2008. My clients needed me to say—and believe— "We're going to get through this. This is going to end at some point, and we're going to win." By the same token, I sometimes have to talk people down from potentially making bad choices in high-risk investments. The challenge is not to come up with a good strategy. Almost any advisor worth his or her salt can do that; the challenge is to manage emotions and behavior.

Before the game with Kansas, Coach K got his players together and reminded them that they could definitely be beaten. No one is so good that they no longer need to prepare and go into things with the right mindset. If his

> **No one is so good that they no longer need to prepare and go into things with the right mindset.**

team didn't, they'd be out. Fortunately, that didn't happen: they beat Kansas in that game and became national champions.

## WHAT CAN AN ADVISOR DO FOR YOU?

A great advisor can do the same thing for his or her clients as Coach K did for his players. The thing about investing is that it's extremely difficult to do well on your own. There's nothing to feel bad about there; it's true for everyone. Four primary reasons come to mind for hiring an advisor as your investor coach:

1.  An advisor helps keep you focused on what the right decision is over the course of years and through uncertainty and emotional stress.

2.  An advisor can also hold you accountable to your stated goals.

3.  An advisor will help you redirect your fears. It's one thing to know that you're human and have biases and fears, but it's another to actually work through them on your own. An advisor can be completely focused on your goals, even when you, as the investor, struggle to do so.

4.  An advisor is always there. Like a good coach, a good advisor is there through all the ups and downs to make sure that you are successful in the end.

Choosing your advisor is the most important financial decision you'll ever make—not *one* of the most important, *the* most important. I firmly believe that the advisor you choose affects your success as an investor more than anything else. It's tempting to view advisors as interchangeable, as if they were a commodity. That's definitely not the case.

> ## THE THREE PRIMARY KINDS OF ADVISORS
> The three types of financial advisors you'll encounter most frequently are brokers, independent agents, and registered investment advisors.

A broker, sometimes called a registered representative, is paid a commission to sell investment products. This kind of broker essentially brings you into the company for which he or she works. Brokers are very focused on the products they have available for you—sometimes more than they are on you or the specific plans you need to make. Because a registered representative works for a company rather than working for you, they can have difficulty avoiding conflicts of interest.

An independent broker is also available to do investment planning. Although independent agents can do a good job, they can still be very product-focused and are often biased about certain investments and insurance products. They are typically labeled "fee-based," because they charge not only fees but also commissions. They are not always required to act in your best interest.

Fee-only fiduciaries, known as registered investment advisors, or RIAs, are called "fee-only" because their only source of compensation for investment advice comes directly from clients. This is the kind of advisor I recommend the most highly. The fees can be a percentage of assets, flat fees, or hourly fees. Unlike the other advisors, fee-only fiduciaries are required by law to always act in the best interests of their clients for all types of accounts. The difference, to put it simply, is that clients pay for the advice rather than for the products sold. This structure allows an advisor to be objective with his or her advice, which typically produces better results for clients.

# THREE QUESTIONS TO ASK WHEN CHOOSING AN ADVISOR

## 1. IS THIS PERSON HELD TO A FIDUCIARY STANDARD?

Someone held to a fiduciary standard is legally required to put his or her clients first. It's important to understand that independent brokers are not always held to this standard, although the recent Department of Labor Fiduciary Rule did change this for retirement accounts. How can you tell whether your advisor is a fiduciary? Simply ask: do your homework to make sure that your advisor is acting in your best interest.

**If you want to know, you have to ask:**

1. **Do my interests come before other interests?**
2. **Can you put the fees I will pay in writing?**
3. **What are your credentials?**

## 2. HOW TRANSPARENT IS THIS PERSON'S PAYMENT?

In general, advisors are paid either on commission or through fees. This is important for the client: a lot of people don't even know what they're paying their advisors in fees. In fact, I just read an article in the *Wall Street Journal* in which a journalist sought to find out how much she was paying in fees for her investment portfolio. She had four different advisors look into it and received four different answers that ranged from a few hundred dollars a year all the way up to 2 percent of the total portfolio. After many hours, she was finally able to determine that she was paying 1.4 percent. When hiring an advisor, you should know what you are paying for the portfolio and the advice. If you don't know, or the advisor can't tell you, it's time to find another advisor.

A broker can be paid on commission. The pay structure works like this: You put $100,000 into an investment product. The broker may earn a 5 percent commission for investing your money in this product. Your $100,000 goes into the investment product, and the advisor gets back 5 percent of that or, in this case, $5,000. It's as if you yourself paid him that 5 percent, but a common sales tactic is to tell the client, "Don't worry, you aren't paying me anything—the company pays me." This is not exactly true. Sure, you may not see the $5,000 go directly to the broker, but the product may carry large fees that your portfolio pays annually. This is how the company can pay the 5 percent commission to the broker. Ultimately, you are still paying $5,000 from your account!

With fees, by contrast, a client pays the advisor a predetermined fee directly. It is usually a percentage of assets or a retainer fee, but it's more of an ongoing fee with the expectation of receiving advice on an ongoing basis. It's also completely transparent. The fee goes directly to the advisor, so you know how much you're paying him or her. Registered investment advisors can't be paid on commission— only advisory fees.

An advisor is more aligned with the client's best interests under a fee structure because he or she is getting paid on an ongoing basis to grow your wealth. Under the commission model, the broker has a financial incentive to move your money around needlessly so that he or she can earn more commission for reinvesting your money—

possibly to your detriment. On the other hand, if you're paying your advisor an ongoing fee of 1 percent or less per year, the advisor has no financial incentive to mess with your money needlessly. It's also easier to make changes: the fee percentage remains the same, but if your broker is paid on commission, everything you do with that advisor triggers another commission.

## 3. WHAT ARE THIS PERSON'S CREDENTIALS?

When seeking out an advisor, it's easy to get lost in the alphabet soup that typically follows an advisor's name. There are a jumble of different certifications and credentials, and many of them are pretty worthless. That said, there are three that stand above the rest when hiring an advisor.

**Certified Financial Planner**, or CFP, is probably the most widely recognized designation when it comes to financial planning or investment planning. The certification requires passing six different education courses, including retirement planning, tax planning, financial planning, investment planning, and insurance planning, as well as a course on mandatory ethical codes. It culminates in a very difficult two-day final exam. To maintain this certification, a CFP must attend ongoing continuing education courses. If a CFP does something that wasn't appropriate for a client, he or she will be stripped of the certification. If a potential advisor has gained a CFP certification and is maintaining it, that's a good sign that he or she might be qualified.

**Chartered Financial Analysts**, or CFAs, are much more con-centrated in the investment area, whereas the CFP is a broader cer-tification covering noninvestment topics as well. Earning the title of

CFA has three steps, and most people don't get past the first because of its difficulty. On a global level, however, this is one of the more valuable certifications to seek out in an advisor. It's a good indication that the potential advisor has a high degree of education and will be able to analyze potential investments at a very high level. Ideally, you would like the one managing the portfolios to have this certification or at least be pursuing it.

The **Certified Public Accountant**, or CPA, certification represents a high level of professional accomplishment because of the demanding exams involved in earning it. A CPA who has taken the initiative to also become a personal financial specialist (PFS) is even better trained as a financial planner. CPAs are also very helpful when it comes to understanding the tax code and how that might affect a person's financial and investment plan.

### THREE THINGS AN ADVISOR CAN DO FOR YOU THAT YOU CAN'T DO ON YOUR OWN

- **See things objectively.** Most important of all, your advisor is not you. It is impossible to be impartial about your own plan. Having a second pair of eyes on your financial planning can add more objectivity to your investment plan.

- **Provide needed perspective.** A competent advisor gives you perspective when you need it most. Perspective is a long-term vision of things amid short-term challenges and uncertainty. It's easy to get caught up in short-term problems, but looking at the bigger picture is the key to abundant investing.

- **Help you plan.** Your advisor can help you create a plan and make sure that you stick to it. In short, your advisor can bring much-needed discipline. It's all too easy to go off the rails or spend all your time reacting to current events instead of being proactive in your decision making and planning.

## INVESTING AS A TEAM

It's best to think of fees paid to your advisor not as an expense but rather as an investment having an expected positive return. That's why you should try to pursue the best rather than your brother-in-law or the really slick salesperson. Don't get me wrong—avoiding paying unreasonably high fees is important, but if all you look at is how much you're being charged, you might miss the value you're paying for.

If you choose the right advisor, those fees do pay off handsomely. Paying close to nothing in fees sounds great and all, but if you under-perform the average portfolio by 3 percent even after paying close to zero in fees, you still come out behind. But if you pay a top advisor 1 percent and he or she gets your portfolio to make 3 percent above the average investor return and manage your risk, you're still up 2 percent after fees. It's not what you pay up front: it's what you get for what you pay.

## INVESTMENT BEHAVIOR PENALTY

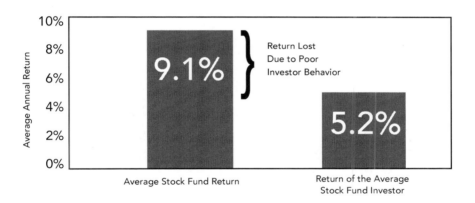

Here's a concrete example of how paying an advisory fee might have helped someone during the most recent major market downturn. Suppose that in 2009, an investor paid an annual fee of 1 percent of the investor's balance to an advisor. If the advisor were able to do nothing more than keep the investor focused on staying within his or her portfolio rather than going to cash, that advisor probably added at least 250 percent investment return from March 2009 to the end of 2016. In this example, over seven years, the investor paid 7 percent total, and, after fees, is up well over 200 percent. The net in that situation was 243 percent. And this doesn't even consider the other ways a great advisor might have added value, such as by rebalancing, reducing taxes, or proposing spending strategies.

Some people will always say, "Hey, I'm not going to pay an advisor and am going to save that money." These are the same people who were at the highest risk of bailing on their plan in 2008 or early 2009 when the market seemed to be going down every day—because they couldn't do the things for themselves that an advisor can do. (See the box "Three Things an Advisor Can Do for You That You Can't Do on your own.") They kept their money in cash and saved the 7 percent, but they made next to nothing on their money. They might have slept well in 2008–2009 by not being invested in the market, but they probably didn't sleep well from 2010–2016 when the markets were recovering!

It's all about the perspective, objectivity, and disciplined planning that an advisor can provide. If your advisor can do those things for you, then he or she is going to be an incredible bargain for what you pay. Don't miss the forest for the trees.

> **It's all about the perspective, objectivity, and disciplined planning that an advisor can provide.**

# TEAM PLAYING: FIVE WAYS TO BUILD A BETTER RELATIONSHIP WITH YOUR ADVISOR

---

**FIVE WAYS TO PLAY WELL WITH YOUR ADVISOR**

1. Form a high-trust relationship

2. Be coachable

3. Set reasonable expectations for yourself

4. Communicate with your advisor

5. Understand and study the history of markets

---

**First, invest trust.** For a good relationship with an advisor to grow, you need a lot of mutual trust. When you find the right advisor, you should be able to trust him or her, knowing that he or she is confident and understands you and your goals. *Never* hire an advisor whom you can't trust. Certainly trust must be earned, and you're going to have some questions along the way. You're going to have fears and emotions, and you'll bring those to your advisor. Over time, you'll find that you can't maximize the value that an advisor's going to bring to you if you're listening to multiple—often conflicting—opinions.

Taking on outside opinions would be like those Duke players' listening to Coach K and then saying, "But I was talking to my Dad or this other coach too, and they had this point about the game." When this happens, neither you nor your advisor can reach your full potential. This seems like a basic concept, but some people just don't heed it. In addition to finding a trusted advisor, it's also very important to be a good client. You need to be able to trust your advisor if you are going to have a successful relationship with him or her. An easy way to get a jump on that is by getting a referral from a respected mentor, a colleague, or your CPA or attorney.

> **In addition to finding a trusted advisor, it's also very important to be a good client.**

**Great investors are coachable.** A good athlete is someone who is coachable. Coach K actually talked about Michael Jordan when he worked as a staff member for the 1992 Olympics USA team, the famous Dream Team that also included Magic Johnson and Larry Bird. Jordan, of course, is widely considered the greatest basketball player in the history of the NBA— the player my generation talks about as the measuring stick for all other players. Coach K said, Michael Jordan in 1992, already having climbed to highest mountain in the NBA, was incredibly coachable, was always trying to get help on how to win the game. He said that Jordan was always looking to get coached more than any other player on the Dream Team, even though he was already the best one on the team. Michael Jordan's "coachability" might well be the reason he was the best.

**Get real.** It's also important to have reasonable expectations. You and your advisor need to talk about them so that you can be on the same page and reach realistic goals. If you're thinking you're going to earn a 10 percent annual return without any potential downside or volatility, that's not a reasonable expectation. Having the right expectations is incredibly important for the relationship to be successful.

Your advisor can help set reasonable return expectations after he or she understands your willingness to handle volatility.

**Just talk.** Communicate freely with your advisor. Be open about your expectations and motivations. Your advisor may be able to read a profit-and-loss statement, but that doesn't mean your advisor can also read your mind. Make sure to keep your advisor apprised of important events in your life, such as the addition of a family member, a house sale or purchase, or anything else that might affect your plan. My rule for clients is for them to stay on the safe side and tell me anything that might be important for me to know. There is no such thing as overcommunicating with your advisor.

**Finally, learn from the past.** An advisor can help you, but you shouldn't be too surprised when stocks go down—and they're going to go down, at some point, while you own them. Almost like clockwork, every year, the market's going to go down at least 10 to 15 percent. You can't go in thinking it's not going to happen: it is, and you'll need to ignore it when it occurs because it won't really matter over the course of your lifetime. I like the way Sir Winston Churchill put it: "The farther back you can look, the farther forward you are likely to see."

## S&P 500 INTR-YEAR DECLINES
## VS CALENDAR YEAR RETURNS

Despite average intra-year drops of 14.7% annual returns
positive in 25 of 33 years

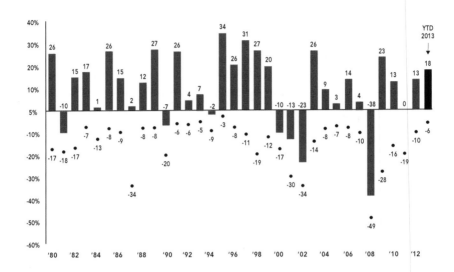

# HOW YOUR ADVISOR
# CAN ADD VALUE

I'm hoping that you already have some idea of what kinds of things I'm going to say here. There are a lot of ways an advisor can add value, but the following, to me, are the most important ones:

1.  The most fundamental way an advisor adds value is simply by getting you a better return after his or her fees than you would have gotten on your own. If an advisor has improved your investment performance and investment plan after you've paid the 1 percent, thus leaving you in better shape than you would have been

on your own, then that's a pretty good indication that your advisor is more than earning his or her pay.

2.  An advisor can also help you with planning on multiple fronts. Plotting realistic goals and timelines is a big one here. An advisor can also help you plan ways to save money on taxes, as well as pointing you toward retirement rules whose potential you can maximize. As Nick Murray says, "there is no financial planning without a financial planner."

3.  Time is the most valuable thing each of us has, and it's also the only asset with which we start on an equal playing field. With a great advisor's services, you'll also save a lot of time—the only finite resource we have. If you're spending a lot of time on your investment planning, and it's taking time away from your family, your spiritual life, your business, or your ability to stay healthy and have fun, then an advisor will be able to help you create a lot of precious time. I don't know whether you can put a specific value on this, but I do know that extra time is a key to abundance.

Advisors can also help connect you with other important partners, serving as the quarterback of your team when needed. Your advisor may be able to recommend a CPA, an attorney, a banker, or an insurance agent. Although the internet has made it easier to find good professional services, if you work with a trusted advisor, he or she may be able to save you some time by referring you to another professional whom he or she trusts.

# THE NONABUNDANT WAY
# VERSUS THE ABUNDANT WAY

| THE NONABUNDANT WAY | THE ABUNDANT WAY |
| --- | --- |
| Never fully trust your advisor; constantly seek out opinions that contrast with his or her advice. | Carefully select the best advisor for you, finding one whom you can trust. See the fee as an investment on which you will receive a great return. |
| View all advisors as commodities; focus only on the fees you might pay. | Understand that a great advisor's fee will be worth many times what you pay. |
| Don't bother to communicate with your advisor about events in your life and changes to your financial picture. | Communicate openly with your advisor. |

# CHAPTER 9

# THE SULLENBERGER LESSON: HOW TO PLAN FOR THE UNEXPECTED

*Plans are nothing; planning is everything.*
–Dwight D. Eisenhower

I once had the opportunity to hear Captain Chesley "Sully" Sullenberger speak: As you may know, he is the pilot who miraculously landed a plane in the Hudson River and saved 155 lives after it encountered a flock of geese on takeoff. Flight experts concluded after the "miracle on the Hudson" that the odds of accomplishing it were incredibly low. Perhaps Captain Sully was the only pilot who could have pulled it off. Unquestionably he is a skillful pilot—but I think there was more to it than that.

After hearing Captain Sully speak, I had the opportunity to talk to him a little, as did other members of the audience. His big takeaway for us was that he did what he did because of a lifetime of preparation. In his case, his goal was to get the plane safely landed. But many things had to happen for that to be possible—and the first thing was to realize that emergencies happen without warning.

Had Captain Sully not been able to safely land Flight 1549 on January 15, 2009, as many as 155 people could have perished. In reflecting on his story, I realized the point: not that he's a superstar pilot who had an incredible stroke of luck, but rather that he diligently prepared for that moment his entire life.

Captain Sully never stopped seeking out safety training throughout his long career. It had to have been very tempting for him to skimp on training, knowing that the odds of encountering such an emergency were incredibly slim. But he was so disciplined that he saw value in safety training even when he knew he might never need to use it—and so when an emergency came, he was able to stay calm. He had about three minutes to put together a plan, and he did. Through his leadership, his crew also remained calm enough to help execute it, and his incredible landing will be remembered for years to come.

There are some strong parallels here with being a great investor: You need to keep a clear perspective and not make rash and emotional decisions, especially during turbulence in the markets. Every day can be an emergency if you make it one. Captain Sully wanted to land his plane safely, much the same way we want to invest and do well. Sullenberger didn't plan to strike a flock of geese that day, but he did plan for a lifetime to respond correctly if it happened. Similarly, for an investor to achieve abundance in the retirement years, it takes a lifetime of planning—with the help of an advisor, of course.

# A SENSE OF HISTORY

There's really only one important prerequisite to good planning: you have to have a basic understanding of history. All too often, people take far too shallow a view of events. As Daniel Kahneman, winner of the Nobel Prize for behavioral economics, has said, "Nothing in life is as important as you think it is while you're thinking it." I can certainly relate to this statement. When trouble strikes, it's not as important as it seems at that moment, but we vastly overestimate its importance for the long term even so. That's just human nature. If you study history deeply enough and far enough back, you'll be able to learn from the past things that help you make better decisions in the future. As Harry Truman says, "the only thing in this world you don't know is the history you don't study."

# THE DOS AND DON'TS OF PLANNING

There are a number of things to bear in mind when making a financial plan. Here are the five most important things *to do*, and the three things that you really need *to avoid*, when making a financial plan:

# DO . . .

1.   Have a concrete financial goal. This needs to be extremely clear, and it needs to drive your investment decisions. Don't start investing until you understand

what your purpose for the money you will invest is and what your overall goal is.

2. Figure out how much cash you need for the short term. (The short term, for our purposes, is anything shorter than five years.) Cash is simply irrational to hold for long-term investing because it will lose money through inflation, but cash is king in the short term for everything from emergencies to large anticipated expenses such as replacing a car.

3. Have a debt management plan. If you have credit card debt with a double-digit interest rate, you shouldn't even be investing long term. You need to get that debt paid off because you can't consistently earn that rate of return through your investments. Even relatively good debt at low rates, such as mortgage debt, needs to be paid off by the time you retire. Ignoring the liability side of your balance sheet will cost you if you don't manage it. You will also sleep much better when stocks go through downturns.

4. Get adequate insurance coverage to address any major risks. During your working years, your biggest asset is not your portfolio, your house, or any of your investment accounts; it's your ability to keep earning income. Make sure that you have appropriate coverage, including life insurance and disability insurance, because if something happens, all your investment planning won't help. Your advisor can refer you to an insurance expert, if need be, so that you or your family can still achieve abundance if something unexpected

happens, such as a premature death or the onset of a major disability. You also need to make sure to have adequate coverage on your home and automobiles, then backstop these coverages with an umbrella policy.

5.  Have a plan to minimize taxes. The goal here is to avoid unnecessary taxes, not evade taxes. Evasion is illegal and will land you in a world of trouble. But it's a good idea to plan in such a way that you can reduce the impact of taxes on your accounts. Your advisor should work closely with your accountant to minimize taxes and maximize after-tax wealth.

# DON'T . . .

1.  Use economic forecasts to guide your investment decisions. Economists are notoriously bad forecasters. For example, in 2009, when the economy was in shambles, many forecasters predicted that everything would continue to get worse. But from 2009 through 2017, we have had one of the best recoveries in stock market history. A lot of people stayed in cash instead of investing in stocks, largely because they listened to these forecasters.

2.  Overreact to short-term performance. In 2008, emerging markets were the worst-performing asset class. They lost over 50 percent in one year—and in 2009, returns were up almost 80 percent. Had you reacted to that performance in 2008 by getting out of emerging market stocks, you'd have missed out on that incredible

recovery only a few years later. Don't overreact to one year of poor performance: it's meaningless in the long run.

3.  Worry about what's hot in the investment world. Whether chasing internet stocks in the late 1990s, real estate in the mid-2000s, or oil and gas in the 2010s, people get badly hurt by jumping onto bandwagons. There will always be the latest hot investments, but when everyone's into it, you know the end is nigh.

# FINE-TUNING AND REBALANCING

Even when you have the right investment plan, you also need a good rebalancing plan. There will be times when parts of your portfolio will really shine and others just won't do as well. There will also be times when things get out of hand: large-cap growth stocks in the late 1990s were a good example of this. Had you bought a well-diversified equity portfolio in the early to mid-90s, you might have initially had a target of holding 20 percent in US Large-Cap Growth. Due to the tech boom, you might have seen this 20 percent target blow up to around 40 percent of your portfolio by the late 1990s. This was the ideal time to think of selling some of those pieces of your portfolio and buying some of the other pieces of your portfolio that hadn't done well. Many people not only didn't rebalance and sell US large-cap growth, but in fact bought more (remember the inverse relationship between risk and return we discussed earlier?) As a result, they were hurt much worse when the tech party came to an end in 2000.

Think of your investment plan like a car: sometimes your tires may need to be rebalanced because one tire may be underweight or overweight. Rebalancing of your investments also needs to be done regularly, but it needs to be done based on predetermined criteria and needs to be disciplined—for example, on the same date every year, or when a given asset class goes down by a given percentage. It's not about timing the market; it's about making sure your investment plan is not out of balance.

Rebalancing is worth mentioning because it is one thing that investors commonly overlook. By themselves, investors have a very hard time being disciplined when it comes to rebalancing. As you should by now expect, this is when the advisor makes sure the client stays disciplined. Multiple studies have found that rebalancing increases your odds of investment success. What's more, rebalancing can reduce your risk of getting hurt worse when bad markets come and can actually enhance your return to some degree. Done well, rebalancing has little downside.

# THE NONABUNDANT WAY VERSUS THE ABUNDANT WAY

| THE NONABUNDANT WAY | THE ABUNDANT WAY |
|---|---|
| Learning history is for high schoolers. | Study history, learning from it to help you be more successful. |
| Rigidly make a plan, then never revisit it again. | See planning as an ongoing process that periodically requires adjustments. |

# CHAPTER 10

# FINDING ENOUGH:
# A CHANGE FOR
# THE BETTER

*The rich invest in time, the poor invest in money.*
—Warren Buffett

## THE STORY OF JOHN AND JACK

John D. Rockefeller and John "Jack" Bogle are two of the greatest minds in business history. They were both incredibly successful, and their stories make for an interesting contrast.

Ron Chernow's biography of John D. Rockefeller, *Titan*, is an interesting and entertaining work of history. I learned a great deal by reading it, including business principles that are still relevant today. Rockefeller was the founder of Standard Oil, which is the predecessor of just about all of the big boys in the global energy space: giants such as Exxon, Chevron, Texaco, and more all came from Standard Oil. Indeed, Standard Oil was so successful and powerful and ran so many companies out of business that it was eventually broken up in the early 1900s by antitrust lawsuits spurred on by Theodore Roosevelt.

Rockefeller is considered to have been the wealthiest American of all time, as well as arguably the most successful businessperson in the history of the United States. When he passed away in 1937, his assets were equivalent to 1.5 percent of the United States' total economic output, a mind-boggling figure. If we factored in inflation, in today's dollars, his net worth would be around $340 billion—more than four times the current net worth of the richest person in the world today, Jeff Bezos.

To his credit, Rockefeller became a charitable person later in his life, funding several large nonprofit organizations. But he was also known to some as a greedy and evil person—both because he was so wealthy and because of how he had acquired that wealth. He didn't always do himself any favors in the reputation department, either: famously, when asked how much was enough, he replied, "Just a little bit more."

John "Jack" Bogle is the founder of Vanguard, the largest mutual funds company in the world. He's very well known in investment circles—perhaps more than anyone other than Warren Buffett. even now, at 88 years old, he is still as sharp as ever. After founding the Vanguard Group in 1974, he served as its CEO until 1996. He pioneered the index fund, which created hitherto unimagined opportunities for individual investors to invest their money, building wealth more easily than was possible using the other options available at the time.

Bogle has made a lasting impact on the world of business by improving people's lives, and his legacy has only grown since he stepped down as CEO of the Vanguard Group—which today has more than $4 trillion in global assets and is still growing. Bogle's estimated net worth is $80 million. Certainly that is wealth by almost anyone's standards, but, even so, it is merely a fraction of the fortunes owned by the richest people in the world. This discrepancy comes by Bogle's own choice: during his time at Vanguard, he never sought to maximize his own income. Like Rockefeller, he has also been charitable. Because his net worth is less than that of some of the richest people of our time, he has no great organizations named after him for his financial contributions, but he has been able to improve people's lives regardless.

Bogle wrote a book that he called simply *Enough*. I highly recommend it for exactly this premise: having enough. In it, he recounts the story of when Joseph Heller, the author of the novel *Catch-22*, once attended a party hosted by a billionaire hedge fund manager. Another guest observed that their host made more money each day than Heller would make in his whole lifetime from sales of *Catch-22*. Unfazed, Heller responded, "Yes—but I have something he'll never have: *enough*."

Having enough is a matter of understanding that there will never be enough money for abundance if you're focused only on how much money you accumulate. It's more about understanding the need to reflect on what is sufficient to meet your goals and sufficient to bring you fulfillment in your job and life through the knowledge that you're doing things that matter to you. Financially, having enough is extremely important. After all, that's the premise of the book you're holding. But if you're not careful, you'll never have enough. And if you can never have enough, you can never experience abundance.

The contrast interests me: John D. Rockefeller had untold billions measured in today's dollars—far more than John Bogle will ever have. Yet Bogle was able to make an impact similar to that made by Rockefeller because he knew when he had enough. Having enough doesn't mean having as much money as possible; that can't be the end goal for the truly abundant.

## DUMB THUMBS

As a rule of thumb, I don't believe in rules of thumb.

Often, I hear people's "rules of thumb" about how much money you need to retire. They say, "I heard from my smartest friend that you really can't retire unless you have $3 million dollars"—or $5 million, or more. My reaction is always the same: "You are unique, distinct from everybody else. No one is like you. No one has exactly your same situation. No one has your thoughts on risk. No one has your exact income goals."

What's more, although there may be some similarities between you and your friend, you will never be exactly the same. One person's $2 million might be enough, another one might want $1 million, and yet another one might need $10 million.

# STEPS ON THE PATH TO ABUNDANCE

1. **Know your goal.** How do you know when you have enough? You can follow steps with your advisor to help you find out, but the first and most important step is to *know your goal.* If you know that, then you can start to figure out how much income is required to meet that goal. Even if it's just a ballpark figure, you need to know what it is. If you're 50 years old and your goal is to stop working at age 62, there might be no way of knowing *exactly* what "enough" is—but you can arrive at a reasonably close approximate number. Once you know your goal and have a rough idea of what you need to reach it, you're ready to start taking steps to get there.

2. **Identify more specifically what you need.** The second step is to look at what your *current* expenses are. Look at your budget at that point and what you think will be part of your budget in the future, as well as things that eventually won't be part of your budget any longer. Your daughter won't need braces every year. Eventually, you'll pay off your mortgage. Again, we're looking for a ballpark figure here. Your financial adviser can help lead you in that discussion; the key is coming up with a number.

3. **Remember passive income.** The third step is figuring out your mailbox income—money that will be coming in no matter what you do. As an example, Social Security disbursements will be there in the future. Some

people also have pension plans that will pay a certain amount of money monthly for the rest of their life. Other people are invested in income-producing real estate or other income producing assets like mineral royalties. Regardless, you need to figure out what your mailbox income will be.

4. **Mind the gap.** What's the gap between your income needs and your mailbox income? Suppose you need around $100,000 per year to meet your lifestyle goals. This $100,000 is a pretax figure because there are taxes associated with Social Security and pension income. If you have around $30,000 coming in from Social Security and around $10,000 from a company pension each year, that gives you $40,000 no matter what. You need $100,000, however, so you have a $60,000 gap. We now know that your portfolio needs to produce at least $60,000 of annual income to fill this gap.

## THE 7 PERCENT SOLUTION

I'm going to give you one rule of thumb that I'll admit is worth knowing: the 4 percent withdrawal rule. Here's how it works: Since World War II, inflation has averaged about 3 percent a year. We know that the cost of goods and services will keep going up. (If you need proof, simply look at a postage stamp from 1987: it cost 22 cents and in 2017 a stamp costs 49 cents.) So if you take 4 percent for withdrawal and you factor in 3 percent for inflation, that means that you really need a 7 percent return. You need to earn at least an annual average of 7 percent or greater to make sure that your principal doesn't go down too quickly during your lifetime.

This is an important rule, because—as we've already discussed—the biggest risk for most people is outliving your money. We never want to have a withdrawal rate that pressures our principle to go down too quickly, because if you live a long life—and people are living a lot longer than they used

> We never want to have a withdrawal rate that pressures our principle to go down too quickly.

to—you never want to be concerned about that principal's going down to zero before you pass away. We want to have a withdrawal rate that gives us a high amount of confidence that our portfolio will be able to offset withdrawals and inflation while ensuring that we never run out of money.

To return to our gap example: We need $60,000 to meet the difference. We can calculate that we need $1.5 million invested to generate enough for our withdrawal of $50,000, equal to the safe 4 percent. We want to have that factored in for inflation. What's more, don't count on $1.5 million meeting that need 50 years from now because you'll need more than $60,000 dollars, factoring in inflation, to ensure that your quality of life doesn't go down.

## AN ABUNDANT RETIREMENT

Many people have the opportunity to increase their wealth throughout retirement. If an investor has a portfolio that's invested mostly in stocks, and if he or she is able to take a reasonable withdrawal rate that is still enough to meet his or her goals, then that person can actually increase in wealth throughout retirement. This creates the potential for that person to leave a legacy. What exactly is a legacy? A legacy is personal; it means something different to every person. It may mean making sure that your grandchildren never have student loan debt when they get out of college. Another person might desire to fund a meaningful community project.

Everyone has opinions about money. The cliché has it that money itself is the root of all evil, but money by itself is neither good nor bad. Indeed, the Bible doesn't say that money is evil; rather, it says that the "love" of money is the root of all kinds of evil. Having more money isn't evil. Rather, what can be evil is loving it too much, viewing it as greater than everything else in your life.

Never feel bad about having a big money goal—that's not bad. What could be bad, though, is if you let that put you in a position in which you're constantly putting the acquisition of more above all else. Never feel bad about big goals; just make sure that you're clear on what is enough (see earlier) and then focus on that.

## WHEN SPENDING MONEY IS THE RIGHT FINANCIAL DECISION

Being a financial planner, my natural tendency is not to spend money, which differs from how my wife she sees things. She's not a frivolous spender, but from the beginning, our relationship was always really big on more experiences—fun family events, celebrations, casual get-togethers, and particularly vacations and trips. Early in our marriage, I didn't understand the importance of these experiences. She and I disagreed on how to spend the little bit of money that we had. At the time, my wife was going to law school, and I made very little money. I remember her saying, "Hey, we still need to go on a trip." Every time she did, I thought, *why would we go on a trip when we're barely getting by?*

But the trips we have taken, even the ones we took during those penny-pinching days early in our marriage, have been some of our best experiences. As time went by, even when we had larger budgets, we still tried to save like everybody else, yet even after having kids, we still made a point of prioritizing vacations. Every year, we invest— and yes, it is an investment—in a fairly substantial vacation for our family, then another one for just me and my wife.

Sometimes spending money *now* instead of later really is the best financial decision you can make because it's all about balance. If you are sticking with your abundance financial plan, you never want to get in the mindset of *I can never have enough*. In some circumstances, spending money can actually be the best investment for you because there are opportunities now that you may never get back in the future.

> **Spending money can actually be the best investment for you because there are opportunities now that you may never get back in the future.**

## MEMORY VERSUS POSSESSION

You will notice I said that spending money can be a smart financial decision—but that spending is on *experiences*, not *things*. The evidence from psychological research is clear: positive experiences bring more happiness than possessions do.

Almost as important as your own age when you undertake these experiences are the ages of your kids or your grandkids. At some point, my kids are not going to be fired up about traveling with Mom and Dad. You've got to seize these opportunities. If you're on track financially, make sure you do. And if you're not on track financially, remember: you can still create memorable experiences on a budget. I'm not advocating frivolous spending. Rather, I'm saying that if you're in a financially stable place, part of achieving abundance is knowing when to invest in your life, not just your accounts.

## THREE STEPS TO INVESTING IN EXPERIENCES

1. Have a financial plan and stick to it. Before anything else, you've got to be on track to meet your long-term goals.

2. Save far ahead of time. Sometimes you have to delay an experience, but doing so can add to the building anticipation and let you solidify your finances so that you can enjoy every minute of it without worrying. Start a separate account to save for big things you want to do, whatever they may be.

3. When you do embark on your adventure, go all in on it. Avoiding cutting corners can help you get the most out of your time. Remember: sometimes it's better to spend an extra $1,000 now instead of later if this experience won't be available down the road.

One of my favorite clients is within five years of retirement. He has plenty of wealth to retire, as proven by his retirement projections—thanks to the incredible job he has done of saving and investing. He and his wife's 25th wedding anniversary was drawing near, and she had been bugging him (for a long time, actually) about taking a big trip together. They have three adult kids now, but that hasn't made him any less of a penny-pincher. When their 25th anniversary came around, he decided to go all out: he took his wife and his three kids to Aruba. He did not hold back on cracking open his wallet—which was not like him.

I saw him a few weeks after he got back, so of course I asked about the trip. With great excitement, he told me that it was probably the best experience he'd ever had in his nearly 60 years of life. He said, "I wouldn't trade that for anything. I'm so happy to see my family laugh about it and talk about it." I was unendingly pleased to hear him say that. His $10,000 "investment" had brought a greater return for his abundance than any security or mutual fund ever could have.

If you're on track or ahead of the game, why wouldn't you give yourself permission to do this? That trip might end up having been the best experience of my client's life no matter how long he lives. Why wouldn't you want to give that to yourself and your loved ones, too? I've been advising others long enough to know that sometimes people routinely miss opportunities to enjoy their wealth. My mission is to be the friend that nudges them to spend the $10,000 they can afford, rather than pad their big pile of money.

Here's a quick story that might give you the nudge you need if you struggle with spending money on worthwhile experiences. My wife lost her dad when he was 49 years old. He was great at giving them these awesome experiences when she and her sisters were growing up, and she still talks about him and these experiences to this day. The hole left by his death would have been even deeper and more sorrowful had he never shared these unforgettable experiences with his four daughters. We are not promised tomorrow, so when those opportunities come, we don't want to miss them. In the Bible, Solomon observed that the wise have wealth and luxury because they plan ahead, but he also talked about living life while you are living life. That's my goal, and I hope it's yours, too. After you achieve your abundance retirement goal, that isn't the time to focus only on acquiring more money. Your retirement is when you get to spend, enjoying the money that you've acquired. If you forget why you started working on your financial plan in the first place, that can be very damaging. No one wants to be lonely, unfulfilled, and adrift after finally achieving an important life goal.

# THE NONABUNDANT WAY VERSUS THE ABUNDANT WAY

| THE NONABUNDANT WAY | THE ABUNDANT WAY |
|---|---|
| Manifest the "never enough" syndrome, even after you have achieved your retirement goals. | Discover how much is "enough" for your goals. |
| Use other people's rules of thumb to tell you whether you can retire. | Annually do the math with your advisor to determine how much you need and how much of a safety net you have. |
| Keep lots of extra unnecessary cash on hand because doing so feels "safe." | Keep enough cash to cover your expected expenses, as well as some extra "sleep well at night" cash—but not so much that inflation kills your plan. |

# CHAPTER 11

# THE WELL-BALANCED SECOND LIFE: MAXIMIZING YOUR LIFE'S POTENTIAL

*If the first half was a quest for success,*
*the second half is a journey to significance.*
–Bob Buford, author of *Halftime*

Lou Holtz was a very successful college football coach who flourished during the 1970s and 1980s. He coached six different college teams and an NFL team, but he was best known for his stint at Notre Dame. He won a national championship with the Fighting Irish in 1988, the year his team went undefeated. Their biggest win that season was the famous "Catholics vs. Convicts" game, when Notre Dame defeated the defending 1987 national champion, the Miami Hurricanes.

Holtz took six teams to a bowl victory and led four different college teams to a top 20 ranking. Obviously, Holtz has been very successful at the coaching side, but he has a lot more to him than just his college football coaching career. In his later years, he has become a college football analyst on ESPN. He also gets paid big bucks for his speaking and leadership training for business leaders. But there's still more to him than that.

**Lou's Little List.** In 1966, when he was 28 years old, Lou Holtz made a bucket list, and he didn't wait until he retired from coaching football to get started on it, either. He wrote down 107 things he wanted to accomplish, then he broke the list down into five different categories:

1.  Things he wanted to achieve as a husband and family member

2.  Things he wanted to achieve spiritually

3.  Things he wanted to achieve professionally

4.  Things he wanted to achieve financially

5.  Things he wanted to do purely for excitement

According to Holtz, he has accomplished everything on his bucket list. He wrote down some big, audacious goals, including some things that others would have thought crazy. He wanted to coach Notre Dame football, win a national championship, meet the pope, be a guest on the *Tonight Show*, and have dinner at the White House. He didn't just happen to have an exciting life, though; he decided to bring that excitement to his own life by being intentional, specific, and purposeful about what he wanted to do.

You need to have your own bucket list as a part of your abundance plan. Your bucket list can start as early in life as you want; the more years you have, the better. What is on your bucket list? Keep it compelling. Consider adding some stuff that's outside the box and that gets you excited. By the same token, if your list is too outlandish, consider adding some practical stuff. What are your financial goals? Do you want to make sure that your kids and grandkids aren't in debt when graduating from college? Maybe you want to give $100,000 to your church or help feed hungry children. Perhaps you want to take your kids or grandkids to Hawaii for a week when they turn 13 years old. The goals themselves aren't nearly as important as getting them down on paper. Write down your goals. Involve your spouse if you're married, and your kids, too.

## WHAT IS ABUNDANCE?

Here's an idea for you: write down ten things that you want to do in the next year. Perhaps you dream of attending a Yankees–Red Sox game, or maybe you want to travel to Rome. If you are married, have your spouse do the same thing. After you have your list of the things you'd like to do, narrow it down to your top five. Then rank them in order, comparing with your spouse to see where they overlap. Choose the top one or two on the final list, and make sure you get them planned!

**The right stuff for retirement.** When you retire, you will need a completely different skill set than you had in your working years if you are to succeed financially. Here's a pop quiz to help you think this through:

1. How will you invest your money the right way to get the income you need to last for 30 years or longer?

2. How do you figure out the right time to claim Social Security?

3. What types of investments do you need to hold?

4. How much cash do you need?

5. How do you handle things when markets get really uncertain?

In the past, you'd have worked harder, but now working harder doesn't make a difference. Making a bad decision with your investment plan when you are working is damaging, but you can usually recover by earning more or saving extra money. In retirement, a bad decision with investments may be devastating. This is when your advisor is most valuable, being objective and providing perspective, experience, and a planning background—helping you get through those things so that you can focus on abundance during your golden years.

# REDEFINING RETIREMENT

During the 1960s, the 1970s, and even part of the 1980s, you could retire at 65 from, for instance, General Motors and not have to save for retirement because you'd have a pension plan that was funded on your behalf. This pension would pay you a guaranteed annuity for the rest of your life.

Back then you might live to age 75, and there might not be a lot to do in your retirement: a good deal of sitting around, a lot of golfing and fishing. People didn't put a whole lot of thought into retiring from something and changing to another thing: you retired and were done. Over the past 20 years or so, that has all changed. Partially, this is because people are living a lot longer, but it's also because people have realized many of their greatest and most influential years need not be in the first half of their life, when they're actually working at a job.

I want you to stop thinking about what retirement looked like in the past. You may have something to retire *from*, but you need to have something to retire *to*. The goal is for you not to be dependent on making

> **People have realized many of their greatest and most influential years need not be in the first half of their life.**

a certain paycheck because you have been saving, investing, and following the counsel of an advisor—but you still need *something* to retire to so that you can truly enjoy this part of your life. Perhaps you always wanted to make a contribution of time to your church or to a nonprofit, or maybe you want to volunteer to build a clinic in the remote jungle, or just spend time traveling with your grandchildren.

Whatever it is, you need to find something to retire to, something that provides meaning to you. *You always need a purpose that gets you jumping out of bed each day.*

## WHAT WILL YOU DO NOW?

Now that you're not working a job 40 to 60 hours a week, what will you retire to? Here are just a few of the life-changing things that I've seen people do after retiring from their first phase of life.

**Mentoring** is a great option. If you had a certain line of work in which you excelled, whether you were a doctor, an entrepreneur, an entertainer, a welder, an architect, or a lawyer, then you've got something incredible to offer someone younger than you, something that is nothing less than an invaluable resource: your experience. What's more, mentors often get more out of mentoring than the mentees do.

You might have opportunities to **teach**. Schools and colleges are always looking for people who have certain experiences and backgrounds and who can also pass along that knowledge. You might also consider tutoring opportunities. When you have extra time, you can pour it into these things. You're not tied down by having to earn a certain amount of income, and you don't have to watch the clock because time is more plentiful now. If you've done what we've talked about in this book—if you've saved, planned, and invested the right way—then you have the time and the financial freedom to invest in others. I myself know people who have made this a part of their second half of life and who absolutely love it.

**Family life** is a great option. You can get involved with your family members, including your kids and grandkids, seeking out every opportunity to be there for them. One of my mentors, who is a grandparent, told me that his goal was to be more interesting than his grandkids' friends. He saw the friends as his competition! Why wouldn't you try to really get to know your grandkids, showing them the real you? When you're working, you don't have the time to be at every single game or event. When you're not working, you can be there every single time if you want to. I don't know of anyone who would ever regret spending more time with his or her family.

**Get out of town.** Maybe you've always wondered what it's like to live in another city. I myself would like to live in New York and San Diego someday, when my kids are out of the house. I'd like to rent a place for maybe six months and live in one of my favorite places, something I couldn't have done when I had commitments at my home in Oklahoma. Or you might try a pilgrimage. It's more than just going from A to B: it's slow and thoughtful and quite rewarding.

**Do what I did.** Write a book. Don't worry if your book doesn't sell a lot. Who cares? You wrote a book, and that's something that is hard to find time for when you're always working. At a minimum, you can pass on your beliefs and thoughts to those who come after you.

These are just a few ideas. You're limited only by your own imagination. By being intentional during the second half of your life, you can create some true abundance.

# A SUCCESSFUL RETIREMENT

Having a full, abundant life in retirement is all about finding balance. You need to be smart, and when opportunity is there, you need to take it. Obviously, when you have more time and financial independence, you can capitalize on such opportunities even more.

**Only you can define what "success" means to you. The average person never takes time to answer this question:** *What does success look like for me?* **But don't you think it makes sense to invest some time to get this right?**

**Success is finding fulfillment.** We know that people who stay active and engaged live longer after retirement—and, moreover, are happier. Everyone needs to get involved with something and have something to look forward to, perhaps even more work in retirement. But such work will be optional, which allows you to work at something you enjoy: money is no longer an object.

**Success is reaching a goal every single day.** It might be an audacious objective, or it might be getting the tulips planted, but every day is a microcosm of a universe filled with investment possibilities. Invest in every day with wisdom and patience. Stick to your plan every day, connecting your daily goals to your weekly goals, and those in turn to your monthly goals—and so on. The way you live every single day can reflect a healthy, intelligent approach to investment.

**Success is considered the accomplishment of an aim or purpose.** From a purely financial perspective, it can also be defined as "the getting or achieving of wealth, respect, or fame" through your work. Whether we like it or not, that's where we build success. When

I talk to the fruit guy at my regular grocery store, he exudes enthusiasm for his work. When I ask him a question about a particular fruit or vegetable, he jumps to help me. You can tell his work is important to him. For all I know, he is retired and doing it because he loves it—or perhaps he has a house full of hungry mouths who want to eat something besides fruit. Either way, I bet he feels successful.

**Success is a profoundly individual metric.** Moving from focusing solely on what you need to do to achieve your goals to finding a greater purpose for your life can be very difficult, but it is extremely worthwhile. Here's a question you can ask yourself: what impact do you want to make for generations to come? With your extra time, take an entire day or week to answer this question.

Perhaps you want to make sure everyone in your family goes to college and comes out debt-free. If so, then build that into your investment strategies. You might also set an age at which to talk to your grandchildren about debt and investing. Take your financial advisor with you so that they can learn about compound interest and the Rule of 72.

You'll also have opportunities to impart your wisdom and your values to future generations. Some of this impact we're talking about you can make through finances, but you can also do so through intangible things. Perhaps hire a videographer to follow your family on a fun retreat to the lake, taking videos of the weekend. You can use these videos to discuss your life story and the values of your family. Generations to come will be able to know what you and your family are all about.

If you do it right, you have a great opportunity to make an impact that is felt long after you are gone, including by people who are born after you're gone. That is worth pursuing: moving from success that is all about you and your accomplishments to real significance. No matter how you plan to go about it, you need to consider how you can have a lasting impact.

It has been repeated many times since Socrates first said it, but "the unexamined life is not worth living" because it has not been lived well. It has been lived without the awareness that every moment contains an abundance of possibilities, each worth an investment. Think about somebody who just goes through life, never stopping to admire the abundance so close at hand or filling the night sky. That person has not only missed opportunities for investing each moment with meaning, but has missed life itself.

Simon Sinek, in his book *Start with Why*, refers to people such as Martin Luther King Jr. and Steve Jobs, urging that really understanding the *why* behind things makes all the difference in the world. If you just go along in your life, not considering why you're doing things, how can you make an impact? This is worth thinking about— making sure of your purpose not only when you're working but also, and indeed especially, when you stop working and retiring. You need to think about how you're using your time. Time is finite, so it must be used wisely.

If I get to 60 years old and if I decide to stop working, then in our modern world, I will likely live into at least my mid- to late 80s. That's 25 years multiplied by 365 days. Would it not make sense to take one of those days, or even a couple of them, every once in a while to think about my *why*, and to examine whether I'm spending my time on the things that I'm going to be happy with at the end of my life? Don't be a robot: don't just follow a routine and never think about it.

# THE NONABUNDANT WAY VERSUS THE ABUNDANT WAY

| THE NONABUNDANT WAY | THE ABUNDANT WAY |
|---|---|
| Think small and never think outside the box. Never plan out anything for the second half of your life. | Dream big. Create a bucket list, and make it fun. The earlier you start, the better. Set a crystal-clear vision for yourself and the second half of your life. |
| See retirement as being only for sitting around, playing golf, and traveling. | Use your retirement years to take that pilgrimage, to mentor, to teach, or to work at that dream job. |

# FINAL THOUGHTS

You made it to the end—congratulations! This book was not meant to be like most personal finance or investing books, which overload readers with information. Instead, I was thinking of the 80/20 rule, also known as the Pareto Principle, when I wrote this book: 80 percent of effects come from 20 percent of causes. In this same spirit, I believe that understanding this book's topics will be the 20 percent that gives you 80 percent of what you need to know for investing for abundance. It should also serve as a framework for how you make all your investment decisions going forward. Here is a brief recap of the concepts we've covered in this book:

1.  Never ever invest money without creating a goal for it.

2.  Stocks historically have had two to three times the real return of bonds: they are the key to investing for abundance.

3.  Stop trying to avoid all risks. That's not possible. Instead, identify the biggest risks, then take the necessary steps to manage or avoid them.

4.  Don't make the common mistake of underestimating how long you may live. You probably need to invest in more stocks than you think and for longer than you planned. Most people's biggest risk is outliving their money, not losing their money in stocks.

5.   Know what real diversification looks like, and remember that you should always hate *something* in your portfolio. (If every position is going up, you're not diversified.)

6.   Don't confuse activity for achievement in investing. Look for excitement *outside* your investment plan, and keep investing boring but profitable so that you can live an exciting life.

7.   Remember what Warren Buffett said about market forecasts, and ignore them—*all* of them.

8.   The most important investment decision you will ever make is whom you choose for your advisor.

9.   Gaining perspective and studying history will help you be disciplined, avoiding big investment mistakes.

10.   Find your "enough" number so that you can avoid the disease of never having enough. Also, get used to the idea that sometimes spending money is a great financial decision.

11.   Use the second half of your life to establish your legacy. Don't retire from your job until you know what you are retiring "to."

To get the most out of this book, it's crucial that you take action on the ideas that really stand out to you. First, implement the one idea that truly appeals to you. Perhaps you need to shift your paradigm for how you view stocks as part of your retirement plan, or maybe you aren't sure that you have the right advisor, one whom you can trust to guide you. Whatever it is, take action on that one thing now, before you let any more time pass.

I wish you all the best as you implement your plan to invest for abundance. Please reach out to me if you'd like to pass on any of your own comments about this book or if I can help you along your own path to abundance.

Kendall King

castleviewadvisors.com

kendall@castleviewadvisors.com

# RECOMMENDED BOOKS TO HELP YOU FURTHER PURSUE ABUNDANCE

*Simple Wealth, Inevitable Wealth,* by Nick Murray: This book will convince you (if you aren't already convinced) to buy and hold stocks for your lifetime.

*The Investment Answer,* by Dan Goldie: This book will help you learn the fundamentals of how to build a portfolio, including the asset classes you should consider and the ones you should avoid.

*Halftime,* by Bob Buford: This book is a must-read if you are in your 40s or older. It will help you learn the set of skills needed to be successful in the second half of your life—which are different than those needed for the first half.

*The Rational Optimist,* by Matt Ridley: This book will make you an optimist about the future if you are not already. I can't recommend it highly enough.

*Why Smart People Make Big Money Mistakes and How to Correct Them,* by Gary Belsky: This book is the best I've read on the subject of avoiding bad money decisions.

*Capitalism and Freedom,* by Milton Friedman: This book will help you better understand capitalism and free markets, which are both critical to having a successful long-term investing mindset.

*The Richest Man in Babylon,* by George Clason: This classic book should be required reading for every young person starting his or her career. The author uses parables to communicate monetary principles that are easy to understand.

# ABOUT THE AUTHOR

Kendall King is an independent financial advisor and the CEO of Castleview Wealth Advisors, a fee-only investment advisory firm that provides conflict-free investment and wealth management advice.

Kendall has over 15 years of experience advising clients across the US on a wide range of financial planning and wealth management topics. He graduated from the University of Oklahoma in 2000 with a major in finance and a minor in accounting. He also attained the Certified Financial Planner ™ (CFP®) designation in 2005.

Kendall lives in Oklahoma City with his wife, Courtney, and their two children, Austin and Tanner.

# SOURCES

PAGE 24: Source: Dimensional Fund Advisors

PAGE 26-1: Data provided by Bloomberg. Market cap data is free-float adjusted and meets minimum liquidity and listing requirements. Many nations not displayed. Totals may not equal 100% due to rounding. For educational purposes; should not be used as investment advice. China market capitalization excludes A-shares, which are generally only available to mainland China investors.

PAGE 26 -2: Data is from Bloomberg Barclays Global Aggregate Ex-Securitized Bond Index. Index excludes non-investment grade securities, bonds with less than one year to maturity, tax-exempt municipal securities, inflation-linked bonds, floating rate issues, and securitized bonds. Many nations not displayed. Totals may not equal 100% due to rounding. For educational purposes; should not be used as investment advice. Data provided by Bloomberg.

PAGE 28: In US dollars. Indices are not available for direct investment. Their performance does not reflect the expenses associated with the management of an actual portfolio. Past performance is no guarantee of future results. US Small Cap Index is the CRSP 6–10 Index; US Large Cap Index is the S&P 500 Index; Long-Term Government Bonds Index is 20-year US government bonds; Treasury Bills are One-Month US Treasury bills; Inflation is the Consumer Price Index. CRSP data provided by the Center for Research in Security Prices, The S&P data is provided by Standard & Poor's Index Services Group. Bonds, T-bills, and inflation data provided by Morningstar.

PAGE 34: www.standardandpoors.com/ratingsdirect

Page 35: The graph shows various percentiles of the values of the retirement account at the end of any given period. For example, the 25th percentile indicates that 25% of the outcomes in the specific simulation have a value less than or equal to the value of the 25th percentile. Note that the graph does not show the worst-case scenarios. The presented statistical analyses and graphs summarize the performance over time of simulated retirement accounts. The performance and outcomes of the simulated retirement accounts may vary with each use and over time.

PAGE 38: Source: Siegel, Jeremy, Stocks for the Long Run (2014), With Updates to 2016 Past performance is not indicative of future results. For Financial Professional Use Only.

PAGE 50: Source: Bloomberg

PAGE 51: Nick Murray

PAGE 57,58, 59: For illustrative purposes only. Past performance is no guarantee of future results. Assumes all strategies have been rebalanced annually. See Page 1 for allocation information. All performance results of the balanced strategies are based on performance of indexes with model/back-tested asset allocations; the performance was achieved with the benefit of hindsight; it does not represent actual investment strategies. The model's performance does not reflect advisory fees or other expenses associated with the management of an actual portfolio. Model performance may not reflect the impact that economic and market factors may have had on the advisor's decision making if the advisor were actually managing client money. The balanced strategies are not recommendations for an actual allocation. Sources: Dimensional Fund Advisors LP for Dimensional Indices; The S&P data are provided by Standard & Poor's Index Services Group; MSCI data copyright MSCI 2017, all rights reserved; Dow Jones data provided by Dow Jones Indexes; The BofA Merrill Lynch Indices are used with permission; copyright 2017 Merrill Lynch, Pierce, Fenner & Smith Incorporated; all rights reserved. Merrill Lynch, Pierce, Fenner & Smith Incorporated is a wholly owned subsidiary of Bank of America Corporation; Barclays indices copyright Barclays 2017 Citigroup bond indices copyright 2017 by Citigroup. Source: Dimensional Fund Advisors

PAGE 60: In US dollars. Source for 1916 and 1966: Historical Statistics of the United States, Colonial Times to 1970/US Department of Commerce. Source for 2016: US Department of Labor, Bureau of Labor Statistics, Economic Statistics, Consumer Price Index – US City Average Price Data.

PAGE 63: www.data.org

PAGE 74: Illustrative examples. Diversification does not eliminate the risk of market loss.

PAGE 80-1: The S&P data are provided by Standard & Poor's Index Services Group. Performance data represents past performance and does not predict future performance. Indices not available for direct investment. Performance does not reflect the expenses associated with the management of an actual portfolio.

PAGE 80-2: Number of holdings for the S&P 500 and MSCI All Country World Index—Investable Market Index (MSCI ACWI IMI) as of December 31, 2015. Indices are not available for direct investment and their performance does not reflect the expenses associated with the management of an actual portfolio. International investing involves special risks such as currency fluctuation and political instability. Investing in emerging markets may accentuate these risks. Past performance is not a guarantee of future results. Diversification neither ensures a profit nor guarantees against loss in a declining market. The S&P data are provided by Standard & Poor's Index Services Group. MSCI data © MSCI 2016, all rights reserved.

PAGE 81-1: Dow Jones data provided by Dow Jones indices. MSCI data copyright MSCI 2014, all rights reserved. Russell data copyright © Russell Investment Group 1995-2014, all rights reserved. Barclays Capital data provided by Barclays 2014. Citigroup bond indices copyright 2014 by Citigroup. The S&P data are provided by Standard & Poor's Index Services Group. Performance data represents past performance and does not predict future performance. Indices not available for direct investment. Performance does not reflect the expenses associated with the management of an actual portfolio. Source: Dimensional Fund Advisors

PAGE 81-2: The S&P data are provided by Standard & Poor's Index Services Group. Performance data represents past performance and does not predict future performance. Indices not available for direct investment. Performance does not reflect the expenses associated with the management of an actual portfolio. Source: Dimensional Fund Advisors

PAGE 103: In US dollars. Indices are not available for direct investment. Their performance does not reflect the expenses associated with the management of an actual portfolio. Past performance is no guarantee of future results. MSCI data © MSCI 2017, all rights reserved.

PAGE 105: https://www.portfoliovisualizer.com/backtest-portfolio#analysisResults

PAGE 119: Source: Quantitative Analysis of Investor Behavior by Dalbar, Inc. (March 2015) and Lipper, Dalbar computed the "Return of the Average Stock Fund Investor" by using industry cash ow reports from the Investment Company Institute. The "Average Stock Fund Return" figures represent the average return for all funds listed in Lipper's U.S. Diversified Equity fund classification model. Dalbar also measured the behavior of an "asset allocation" investor that uses a mix of equity and fixed income investments. The annualized return for this investor type was 2.5% over the time frame measured. All Dalbar returns were computed using the S&P 500* Index. Returns assume reinvestment of dividends and capital gain distributions. The fact that buy and hold has been a successful strategy in the past does not guarantee that is will continue to be successful in the future. The performance shown is not indicative of any particular Davis investments. Past performance is not a guarantee of future results.

PAGE 124: Source: Standard & Poor's, FactSet, J.P. Morgan Asset Management. Returns are based on price index only and do not include dividends. Intra-year drops from a peak to a trough during the year. For illustrative purposes only. Returns shown are calendar year returns from 1980 to 2012, 2013 numbers represent year to date returns. "Guide to the Markets - US" Data are as of 9/30/13.